Customer Worthy

Practical Books for Smart Professionals from PMP

Now you can equip all your sales, marketing, and service managers with **Customer Worthy**. It will help them introduce new solutions to your existing operations and open the doors for new business development. You may also want to distribute the book to potential customers to engage them in the design and innovation of new services and help them understand the power of this marketing approach and its implications.

A customized edition, with *"Compliments of* **Your Company Name"** on the cover is available with orders of 200 or more copies. Call us toll-free at **888-787-8100** for quotes on quantity orders.

For more practical books for smart professionals, go to our website, **www.paramountbooks.com**.

Customer Worthy

Why and how <u>everyone</u> in your organization must Think Like a Customer

MICHAEL R. HOFFMAN

Paramount Market Publishing, Inc.

Paramount Market Publishing, Inc.
950 Danby Road, Suite 136
Ithaca, NY 14850
www.paramountbooks.com
Telephone: 607-275-8100; 888-787-8100   Facsimile: 607-275-8101

Publisher: James Madden
Editorial Director: Doris Walsh

Copyright © 2010 Michael R. Hoffman

All rights reserved. No part of this book may be reproduced, stored in a retrieval system, or transmitted in any form or by any means, electronic, mechanical, photocopying, recording, or otherwise, without the prior written permission of the publisher. Further information may be obtained from Paramount Market Publishing, Inc., 950 Danby Road, Suite 136, Ithaca, NY 14850.

This publication is designed to provide accurate and authoritative information in regard to the subject matter covered. It is sold with the understanding that the publisher is not engaged in rendering legal, accounting, or other professional services. If legal advice or other expert assistance is required, the services of a competent professional should be sought.

All trademarks are the property of their respective companies.

Cataloging in Publication Data available
ISBN 13: 978-0-9819869-1-3 | ISBN 10: 0-9819869-1-9

This book dedicated to Corrine Hoffman, Mary Hoffman,
John, Sarah, David, and Julia Hoffman,
and James and Dorothy Ruediger.

Contents

Acknowledgements

Many thanks to my customers, mentors, and partners who knowingly and unknowingly helped validate the CxC Matrix design and metrics: Paul Hamilton, Andrew Morrison, Philippe Mauldin, Robert Hall, Burrell Landes, Julie Casteel, David Eckert, Kevin Ryan, Gwen Hall, Nick Jensen, Claudio Marcus, Kari Regan, Evangelos Simoudis, David Raab, Tery Larrew, and Martin and Regina Foy.

Much thanks and gratitude must go to my wife and family for their support in putting up with me as I dissected every customer situation, approaching everyone from salespeople to customer support representatives, to see "how they do things." Thanks also to my mother and in-laws, and much thanks to everyone who shared customer stories.

Special thanks to Sears for the free lawn mower!

Preface

Confessions of an Enlightened Customer
(*by the way—why the heck am I on hold?*)

Confession 1: I started writing this book while on hold with my cell phone company, listening to horrific canned music and hearing this recording every 90 seconds: "Your call is very important to us . . . You can also get assistance online . . . Have you seen our latest —— ?"

It is all about me, the customer

I started writing, "Twenty minutes online . . .now on hold 11 minutes . . . "

So, why am I still on hold? Because it is the only way to resolve my issue regarding the continued incorrect billing for my service, which is now a whopping month-end bill of $1,700. It should have been closer to $40. And the call-holding message keeps telling me: "Your issue can probably be resolved online. Please visit us at XXX.com."

So frustrating. I sketched out the spreadsheet you see below, logging my time waiting for the phone company the same way I would log time for billing one of my customers. Using some generic numbers from my call center consulting days, my frustration grew with every wasted minute because, obviously, no one at the phone company seemed to have any interest in calculating *what a service issue costs a customer.*

Monetize this:

Michael R. Hoffman Investment	My Cell Phone Company
20 minutes preparation +	
20 minutes online +	
20 minutes on hold +	20 minutes call hold time = *free* +
11 minutes customer service rep interaction time =	11 minutes customer service talk time =
My time: 71 minutes @ $3.00 minute	Company time: 11 minutes @ $0.45 minute
My customer cost = $210	Wireless phone company cost = $4.95
customer cost @ $50 hr = $59.16	
customer cost@ $10 hr = $11.43	

Final Resolution 6-Month Cost

My time: 551 minutes	Customer service talk time: 120 minutes
My customer cost = $1,653	Wireless phone company cost: $54

The $100 Billion Problem

I know I'm not alone in my frustration. The CSR on this call was kind enough to remind me, "Sir, we have over 60 million customers to take care of, and now they are waiting behind your call . . ."

Really? After a brief moment of feeling pity for her and the personal burden she carried in supporting 60 million service-inflicted customers, it occurred to me: "What if all 60 million customers were experiencing the same on-hold frustration?" I quickly started my calculation, and the numbers floored me. My wireless phone company was costing its customers $99,180,000,000. That's nearly one hundred billion dollars that customers pay in addition to their monthly bill! And what do we as "customers" get in return? Please hold for the answer . . .

Here is the core customer problem: Companies—not just in the communications industry—don't keep score by customer. At the executive and corporate levels, management does not measure the time customers invest in researching vendors, building their solutions, using services, resolving issues, the efforts a customer makes to assist in problem resolution, or the sacrifices and inconveniences a customer pays. This strategy worked until recently when the World Wide Web gave customers a voice and a platform to speak to one another, news agencies, and prospective customers.

Customer satisfaction surveys—Net Promoter Score, J.D. Power, and other "everything is all right" customer satisfaction measurement methods—miss the point. They are too far away from the customers, the interactions, and the phone call. The "long tail" is on the phone right now. This is "long tail" meets the Pareto Principle.

Key Takeaway: Poor customer experience design is expensive for everyone, but it is most expensive for customers.

This is why the CxC Matrix that you will learn about in this book is so important. It can be used to fix the customer problems and improve service delivery from the moment a customer begins the journey to fulfill a need all the way to product or service disposal.

Poor customer experience leads to incredible expense—not just for companies, but for customers. (At the time of this writing, the wireless phone company's annual report says that it spent $21 billion in "selling, general, and administrative expense.") Even if I discount the cost of my personal experience by 90 percent, it means that my wireless company cost its customers nearly *ten billion dollars* that goes unreported.

The point is that with all of the investments in product development, sales, marketing, and customer service systems, companies continue to waste an unfathomable amount of customer time—waiting for the technician to arrive to load software or install cable, waiting for a salesperson to return a call, waiting for the answer to an emailed question, trying to figure out how to use a product.

Will I ever do business with the wireless phone company again? Reluctantly, I already have.

Introduction

**Executives can hold meetings, engineers can create designs, manu-
facturers can ship state-of-the-art products, and sales people can hit
the streets, phones, the web, the ads. Operators can even "stand by,"
but if a customer doesn't buy, the entire business has failed.**

Imagine that you have had a discussion with your customers at a conference
table. They have told you all about their experience with your products and
service, including how they found and selected you, how they use your products, their likes, and their gripes. Now, what do you do with that information?
This is where *Customer Worthy* comes in. In this book, you will learn a new
nanoscale business model that leverages advances in technology, process
design, and communications to help you chart your course to sustainable
competitive advantage client by client.

The **CxC Matrix** that is introduced on these pages provides a futuristic
view of your business through your customer relationships. In short, it will
help you create a better way. It isn't as futuristic as it seems, though. You
can begin to implement this now, and it will not only make your customers'
lives easier, it also will make your life easier.

In the future you'll see products and services with built-in sensors and
the ability to morph functions, features, services, and resources throughout
the customer's buying cycle from product acquisition to product use to
product disposal. *Customer Worthy* is your company's introduction to the
beginning of nanobusiness and customer management, where every business decision is traceable to its effect on customers.

With the CxC Matrix, each word in each message, each operational instruction in each device, and each clause in each contract can be carefully, surgically, and calculably crafted to meet each customer's preferences and circumstances. Pricing and servicing are precision-designed to meet your company's and each stakeholder's profit margin and business objectives.

Who should read this book?

Every decision maker at your company should read *Customer Worthy*. Each management team should come together to fill out your company's version of the CxC Matrix. This simple exercise exposes strategic conflicts, uncovers low-effort opportunities, and identifies areas to redirect spending—all centered around customer-centric activities. The result is a seismic shift in business direction and strategy, creating a company that is easier to do business with. It empowers managers to do things right but also to do the right things.

On this new frontier, every business needs a map. In an interview with Esther Dyson in *Strategy+Business,* she said, "Without a map, you can't see yourself in context, whether it's physically in space or in relation to all the other people you know. These little changes make a great difference, and then people start asking themselves, "How could things be done better?"

Customer Worthy provides you with just such a map—a framework and set of measures to support your business. Most importantly, this framework will fuel revenue growth and innovation.

Businesses cannot be successful without making their customers successful, and the CxC Matrix depicts customer success across each department and function company-wide.

Customer Worthy gets everyone in your company on the same page regarding customers—defining them, factoring them into decision-making, and measuring business success based on hard customer information.

The Matrix provides a means for all decision-makers to share a conceptual model of this sensor-filled and smart-service design, enabling companies to plot their current business state and evaluate ongoing decisions.

As your company customizes and modifies products and services to secure more business per customer and command greater profit margins, the number of variations and complexities brought about by all of the potential combinations and configurations may outstrip your ability to manage, predict, forecast, plan, and report.

The goal of any new business model and framework must be simplicity —simple enough for all stakeholders to understand their roles and responsibilities. It even needs to be simple enough for customers to collaborate in the design of continuously improving solutions.

Customer Worthy's CxC Matrix presents a business model diagram that is so simple everyone can understand it. At its highest level, this design has an entry point that everyone can participate in and agree on.

Managers—you are not alone

As a business decision-maker, do you feel like you are under a microscope? Do you feel like someone is constantly looking over your shoulder to scrutinize every decision—questioning every outcome or assumption?

Well, that feeling isn't an illusion, and it isn't going away. Business is going through a transformational period where processes and internal decisions are more transparent, where they can be viewed, critiqued, measured, and monitored by a growing audience of internal and external stakeholders, and eventually everyone, including customers.

The CxC Matrix has the ability to expose all decisions, criteria rules, responsible decision-makers, processes, and resources associated with each component of a customer's experience. While the customer uses a product, researches it, shops, or buys, this ultimate transparency envelops his context, environment, situation, values, needs, disposition, conditions, and projections at the time of each decision.

Ninety percent of the technology is available today

The CxC Matrix does not require a major technology overhaul—just a rethinking or an adjustment to add the customer's view and conceptually invite customers to the planning and decision-making table.

Customer Worthy provides a comprehensive and financially rigorous approach for you to manage from a customer-centric perspective. The tools provide you with the ability to connect strategy to execution in a manner that is easy for everyone to comprehend. The CxC Matrix maps system capabilities in a format that helps business and IT managers clearly delineate what is expected and what will be measured.

These tools are designed to overcome the business information technology conundrum. Technology: "What would you like to do?" Business: "What can I do?"

I suggest that marketing managers give Customer Worthy to their technology departments so that they can better understand how to evaluate tools and design systems with customers in mind. They will begin to develop a keen awareness for optimizing customer value.

Technology professionals should give Customer Worthy to marketing and other managers to help them express their needs programmatically and introduce systems thinking to their requests.

As for Customer Relationship Management (CRM) professionals, the CxC Matrix is the ultimate guideline and workbook for every customer contact enterprise-wide. The CxC Matrix can answer the questions that companies spend hundreds of billions of dollars chasing: "What does CRM look like? What is CRM? How do I grow performance per customer?"

The evolution of the CxC Matrix

The CxC Matrix started as a framework for applying artificial intelligence and predictive modeling techniques to customer management and communications systems in a variety of industries. The visual Matrix started as a framework to measure and present the results of complex modeling systems.

Initially it depicted results for stand-alone, departmental, and specific challenges such as pricing, advertising, distribution, product use, and customer service. The resulting success in any one of these areas consistently had an impact on other areas of the company. For example, more customers responded to advertisements, driving up traffic in stores, on the web, and by phone. This grew sales demand and accelerated inventory depletion. All of these consequences were subsequently modeled to depict company-wide impact.

"Customer" quickly became the obvious persistent variable in each model, so "customer" became the vehicle for measuring success from department to department.

As technology advanced and decision cycle times became shorter, the ability to model customers and scenarios as a stand-alone function outside of the business process stream became less desirable. Companies found greater success embedding decision-making in the process stream. Moving expert decision systems and experimentation into the process stream creates tremendous efficiencies in business processes and revenue potential. The CxC Matrix evolved into a multi-tiered method for designing solutions inclusive of customer preferences and value. The tiers presented as templates in this book represent different levels of CxC Matrix maturity, starting simply with Visualize and growing through Analyze, Monetize, Prioritize, and Optimize stages.

CHAPTER 1

My Car Had a Conversation with my House Last Night . . . when My Office Interrupted

Everything is a computer—your car, phone, television, music player, radio, and so on. With the expansion of WiFi, even more common objects will not only be computerized; they will be networked. You know that security doohickey that stores attach to clothes, expensive items, and controlled substances? Imagine your Blackberry and Outlook calendars simultaneously updated and "aware" of new items you have purchased the moment you cross the threshold of your home with times and days that you should take your new prescription, or your calendar automatically reminding you when to take your medication through a text message sent to your car, cell phone, computer, and music player.

Now, imagine that all of the technology that surrounds you—your PC, phone, radio, car keys, PDA, car, television, and the doohickey in the bag—is monitoring your activities and controlling key aspects of your life (depending, of course, on the settings and who set them).

Your phone flashes: "Take X pill." Ignored, your phone flashes and rings five minutes later, "Did you take your X pill today?" You walk into your kitchen past your microwave that is blinking and flashing: "Urgent Message: Prescription."

Customer experience is the next big thing. Inanimate objects are getting smarter. Remember when TVs had dials and clocks had hands? Now, your TV obeys your command and plays the shows you want to see when you want to see them in the order you dictate and without commercials. Look at your bathroom scale. Look at your car. Look at the security tag in the box of aspirin. The experience is different because there is intelligence around the customer, built into everything, constantly shaping the way customers see and interact with the world.

Caller ID, transparency, physical household, and addressability

All customer processes—business, consumer, and government—are subject to overhaul. The vast improvement in cars and computer usability through USB ports points to the ease of computer components and user adoption. It's the emergence of the Trifecta, the next stage of the evolution, where products are speaking to each other on behalf of the customer and are becoming self-configuring based on a customer's profile. This goes beyond the car that adjusts to three users. It speaks to design function with such questions as: "Do I hit a 1, 2, 3 button?" or "Does the seat measure me?" or "Does the car hear a voice command, or does it simply recognize my voice and dimensions and adjust my seat accordingly?"

This type of awareness is one in which people are defined by their devices, and services are configured as their personal network with a digital "fingerprint" representing their various connections, activities, and user preferences. This is the next wave of technology, societal, and business development. It will vastly change the nature of the way products are consumed, repaired, purchased, reused, and resold. This also has tremendous implications for customer privacy, security, and governance.

The emerging business ecosystem is quickly becoming a reality. Early adopters, savvy technology geeks, and children expect technology, communications, and trusted companies to flawlessly work on their behalf with minimal disruptions or inconveniences. In this new environment, information and trust are rationed out to companies that contribute to the customer's network and respect the customer's boundaries. These trusted companies also proactively protect and represent the customer's values and best interests, often without the customer's acknowledgement, but always with the customer's permission.

In this new environment, the customer is regarded as the arbiter of business decisions. The primary criterion for business success is this: Is the result *Customer-Worthy?*

"The Matrix is everywhere. It is all around us, even now in this very room. You can see it when you look out your window or when you turn on your television. You can feel it when you go to work, when you go to church, when you pay your taxes. It is the world that has been pulled over your eyes to blind you from the truth."

—Morpheus, in *The Matrix*

Fast forward to 2018 and the diary of a day in the life of your customer, Neil

(Excerpted from the short story, Evil Twin, *by Michael R. Hoffman)*

Standing on the light rail train, heading into the city, my folder vibrates, and I see the light flashing through the unzipped space in my backpack. Tilting back, I try to glance at the message. The light is green, so it might be home. I reach through the unzipped corner and pull the screen half-out, bending it back just enough to see the address line.

The *Wall Street Journal* I grabbed at the train station must have had an interactive RFID coupon for 30 percent off the new combo meal at the Starbucks across the street from my office.

I double tap the "Y" on the coupon with my index finger, and the confirmation message alerts me to pick up my sandwich at counter 3. The flashing link below the confirmation also displays a message telling me that I have been entered in a contest for a travel mug with an SD chip and wireless connectivity to play videos and news clips. "You must be present to win. Your current odds of winning are 71:1. This could be your lucky day!"

I jog across the street, gnawing at my sandwich, tasting the melted cheese, ham, and a bit of brown paper.

As I approach the lobby, my folder vibrates (I'm sure it flashes), and I hear, "37 days consecutive on-time attendance. 23 more days to a new golf putter, day spa, flowers home, or grab bag gift, care of Human Performance Resources. Would you like to choose your gift now?"

"Oh, crap!" I mutter as I grab for my ear. I forgot to turn off my office earpiece again. I push the toggle back twice. I think that's how I "mute all."

As I walk into my office, I quickly look left and right and softly say, "Holy stubby Santa!" I pause. Nothing. As I grab my ear and fiddle with the toggle, I hear a soft tone in my left ear and an even softer click on my right. "There you go."

I repeat "Holy stubby Santa," and my desk's half-panel wall begins to glow almost completely green. "Looking good," I say out loud to no one. I hear three quick beeps in my left ear, and a soft, female voice whispers, "3 urgent, 6 exec, 13 office messages, 31 unknown."

I plop down in my chair and run my finger across the green screen. Tiny text blurbs pop-up and disappear as my finger moves along. My eyes focus on the red brown blotch just left of the center of the screen. I tap the blotch and spread my two fingers apart to zoom in and open the underperforming area.

The screen light shudders. Then, a list of "recommended actions" appears in a window overlaying the area. The list, numbered from 1 to 6, includes actions and probable outcomes for each item, presented as percentages. At the bottom of the semi-transparent window where "7" would be, the screen highlights "New" and "Other." Hmmm. . . . I quickly drag my finger across actions "1, 2, 3" and hold it. I pause for a second, and the screen flashes "confirm" as the female voice whispers, "Confirm?" in my left ear.

"Confirm."

"Good sign," I think to myself as the lower traffic light-looking gauge has a "97.5%" next to the green signal and "2.5%" hovering between the yellow and green.

"Not bad, 97.5% of processes running on plan 7 months before the big day; 2.5 out of alignment."

I touch the 2.5% and drag my finger to the lower right "Me" button. I can't help but smile as the "Me" pops up "$48K, $6k, $26K," in blue, red, and green respectively, representing my slice of the projected earned bonus, potentially forfeited bonus, and potential group bonus.

7:10 pm: I lean my backpack against the car, and along with the sound of the door lock opening, the car's dashboard screen is already flashing. I slide in and look at the pulsing message. "MUNICIPAL ALERT MUNICIPAL ALERT" is scrolling across my dashboard in red, bold letters against a sky blue background. I tap the screen, and a message flashes in black letters, "Spring Baseball? Justin Y N Hillary Y N Confirm." I quickly tap both "Ys" and "Confirm." "Confirm debit $625 Citi Y N" pops up on the screen, and I tap "Y, Confirm." The screen then flashes some message about verification among 4 registered items blah, blah, blah and a touch box below that says "Accept Not Accept." I tap "Accept" and "Start Car," cleverly using both hands. Nothing happens, and the warning light flashes in synch on the dashboard and the dome light. "External screens must be turned off to start ignition."

"C'mon, you know what I meant!" I holler back. Nothing.

I tap the flashing and enlarged "Screen Off" button then "Start Car."

As I turn to enter the mall on the way home, the car's in-dash, yellow message light flashes quickly, followed by a high-pitched man's voice asking, "Offers? Yes? No?" Just as I say, "Yes," the voice changes to my wife Eve's voice and says "Groceries" in a soft calming tone.

I say, "No groceries" and hear a beeping phone ring tone fill my car, then Eve's real voice, "Hi, Neil. Honey, are you going to be home soon?" Not really paying attention, I respond, "I'm not picking up groceries."

"What?"

I park close to the hardware store and tap "Car Off." Simultaneously, the car windshield screen projects a lightly flashing message "Offers? Yes? No?" to which I say "Yes." Two large buttons then pop up on the screen: "Some" and "All." I say "Some" out loud, and the names and images from stores in the mall from my preferred list pop up. They are numbered 1 to 5. I say, "1, 3" for the grocery store and the liquor store. Another message then pops up with "1. Bank $25 OK 2. Chinese Restaurant $10 OK?" "No," I grunt as I step out of the car.

As I enter the store, I hear a faint voice in my left ear saying "Coupons?"

I realize that I forgot to turn my ear phone off. "No, thank you" I say quickly and tap my phone off.

I just hate being tracked as I go through the store.

The future is now

This "day in the life" excerpt provides a window into an evolved customer-to-company relationship and a set of experiences that in the not-too-distant future will be pervasive, intelligent, highly personalized, multi-device, and multi-member.

The full spectrum of technology used in the excerpt is already available:

- WiFi;

- Bluetooth;

- Encryption;

- Customer profile-driven personalization, self-configuring, rules-driven marketing and sales offer systems;

- Visual business performance dashboards with touch screen reporting;

- Multi-media, network-connected cars; and

- Multi-device coordination and synchronization.

Neil's day depicts a higher evolution of networked customer, where the buyer's experience, activities, environment, human-to-device and human-to-human interactions, movements—and even occasionally thoughts and reactions—are digitally recorded (either by mistake or intentionally) and stored in distributed connectable databases.

How does a company participate in this network? Who is in charge of coordinating the contacts, messages, offers, and customer service? How can marketing and technology work together to make sure the customer is well served at the same time the technology is used effectively and efficiently?

Companies must begin now to plan how they will participate in this interconnected, always-on, highly personalized network and whether it is an option not to participate in a customer's network.

Non-participation probably isn't an option. A company that chooses not to participate in the customer network is today's equivalent of a company choosing not to have a phone. It's worse than not having a website and not using email because the purchase transaction and the execution mechanism will become more tightly linked—like the Municipal Recreation Department transaction in the above example that was extremely convenient. Automatic payment, service, and payment reminders that follow customers around and are delivered through every form of device and medium will become standard practice.

Customers are morphing marketing, customer service, and product usage contacts at light speed. WiFi, intelligent devices, and personal communication networks are seamlessly linked. Your laptop synchronizes to your phone/PDA/GPS, which synchronizes with your car computer and GPS.

Of course all of this information circulating among devices, passing through airwaves, then passed from system to system and company to company, poses a series of new challenges and problems.

Customer promises

The *Evil Twin* excerpt presents a number of service, delivery, and product fulfillment challenges for all of the companies and parties involved. Let's call them customer promises. For example, one of the challenges of the Starbucks' *Wall Street Journal* interactive offer plus sweepstakes entry is coordinating the messages, resources, and products to create a highly successful, attention-getting, impulse offer. The offer's success requires coordination not just across companies but also across devices, media, channels, systems, departments, and functions.

What if Neil shows up at Starbucks window 3, and they don't have his sandwich? What if the worker at window 3 has no record of the sandwich order, which, incidentally, was debited from his account automatically when he walked up to the counter?

No sandwich = a bad experience. Account debited = a worse experience. Spending time to retrace the offer, order, sweepstakes entry, debit, and credit creates a still worse experience for the customer and the Starbucks employee caught in the middle.

And what happens to the *Wall Street Journal* pay-for-performance advertising campaign results? Should Neil's response be pulled out? Just how do you do that when the WSJ system checked that Neil responded . . . and he did?

Is Neil still entered in the contest for the mug?

You might say, "Who cares?" Well, Neil does! And so do the paid sponsors of the mug and advertising promotion who were going to give Neil a mug regardless of the sweepstakes drawing results simply because Neil has a high projected lifetime value for their financial services. They want a piece of Neil's attention, and they funded the Starbucks discount, the *Wall Street Journal* advertisement, the mug design, the delivery, and the service. The mug also ensured that the financial services company could promote its services by sending messages programmed to appear on the mug's screen. The financial services company valued and specifically targeted Neil, and the entire effort was focused on creating a dedicated channel to communicate directly with Neil.

The cost of privacy

In Neil's story, privacy has a price—or a value. In exchange for verification information, customers share personal information with trusted advisors. In fact, it's very likely that a whole new industry will spring up in the personal network identification business with businesses responsible for insuring and monitoring networks, personal data exchanges, commercial transactions, and risk mediation.

As customers and citizens, we will all have to decide whether we want to give up this level of "privacy" in exchange for convenience, entertainment, stimulation, and attention.

How will you configure systems and processes to manage customer demand for personalized offers, logistics, pricing, packaging, delivery, and service? How should you decide which technologies to pursue and which processes to change, adapt, and invest in? What profit gains and cost savings should you expect?

This is the role of the CxC Matrix—a methodology and framework designed to help *you* plot, visualize, analyze, monetize, prioritize, and optimize all customer contacts customer-by-customer and contact-by-contact.

CHAPTER 2

The CxC Matrix Unveiled

Right this minute, your company is missing hundreds of opportunities to grow revenue and reduce costs. Hundreds of assets are being under-used.

Worse yet, these assets are completely paid for, and in the time it took you to read to this word, hundreds more opportunities were lost.

What if you could coordinate the messages across each of the channels for advertising, promotion, sales, and operations? What if the call-waiting message, the "thank you" at the store, the owner's manual, and the welcome letter were all presented as a unified message and single call to action? What would the impact be on the rest of your business?

Contact: Any connection between a customer and a company, its products, services, and partners. The CxC Matrix classifies contacts along two major dimensions: channel and consumer cycle. Consumer cycle reflects the buying cycle of customer needs, attributes, and processes, while channel represents company resources and behavior.

Each contact a customer has with your company, its products, its services, and its partners is an asset and a pivot point for company success. Every interaction has tremendous revenue opportunity, along with enormous risk potential. Yet customer interactions are the most underused asset in most companies.

Most marketers understand the importance of thinking like a customer, but adopting the "Think Like a Customer" mindset probably requires a tremendous shift in many other parts of your company including management, operations, and finance. It's a cultural shift, not a systems upgrade or replacement, not a firing and rebuilding. It's a paradigm shift in mindset, developing an inquisitiveness focused on what we can do better for customers at each contact.

What would the value of a 0.05 percent improvement in customer flow, conversion rate to purchase? What would an additional 0.05 percent increase in referrals do to your bottom line?

What if each individual message was refined and scoped specifically for *every contact,* crafted based on the customer's interests and profile—hitting *each customer's* value-set spot on, making the customer feel exceptional and trusting of your company?

Who could ever compete with you if you had all of that going for you? Who could match your ability to manage the customer experience? This competitive advantage comes from your company's ability to factor the customer's interest into each customer contact, leveraging technology and design to get the highest return per interaction.

Excellent, profitable customer experiences are about winning. Profitable growth and sustainable competitive advantage come from mutual win-wins for the customer, wins for the employee, wins for the company, and wins for its partners and shareholders. Collectively, how do we move this customer further along in the relationship? How do we create urgency across all of the contact points?

The CxC Matrix clearly delineates all of the win points, all of the individual contacts, and all of the desired outcomes at the exact interaction points, including the systems, people, actions, resources, and tasks required to win and achieve success at each stage of the consumer buying cycle. Customer flow—movement across the consumer lifecycle—depicts the degree of customer worthiness from contact to contact.

Customer flow is a barometer for success

Customers vote with their wallets and their feet. Plain and simple, this is the reality underpinning the CxC Matrix: closely manage success in each customer contact, and reap the benefits of more business per customer, achieve higher margins, and grow more customers. The Matrix captures customer flow at its most detailed levels, customer-by-customer and contact-by-contact.

Companies that cannot monitor customer worthiness or see contact flow data are continually surprised by revenue shortfalls, inventory outages, resource cost overruns, and diminished customer satisfaction. Traditional financial measures lag too far behind customer activities to be effective for timely business decision-making. Operations and quality metrics are too far removed from a customer's interests, intent, and preferences. As a result, your company's internal measurements can look fine. Quality and operations metrics can appear good to great. But customer and contact flow may expose disengaged and indifferent customers. The result is revenue decline and business erosion.

The CxC Matrix is designed to help your company quickly find and exploit untapped customer value opportunities while working with existing tools for measurement, decision-making, and planning. The CxC Matrix offers you the ability to integrally weave "customers" into your strategies, planning, and goal-setting.

Despite the use of a variety of business analytics and software, few companies can create a complete view of all customer interactions or manage the customer experience across functions through the customer life cycle. The Matrix is the first approach that relates actual business results with a consistent, end-to-end view of the customer experience. It allows you to measure how changing any aspect of a CxC Matrix contact affects business processes throughout your company.

The CxC Matrix is built from the customer's perspective. While businesses use many forms of buying models and customer life cycle models, the Matrix pays special attention to matching a company's people, systems, information technology infrastructure, and performance metrics to each stage of the consumer cycle and corresponding set of contacts.

Each contact is a battleground

Customer contacts are the new battleground for companies looking to secure more business and fend off competition.

Figure 2.1 Customer Contacts

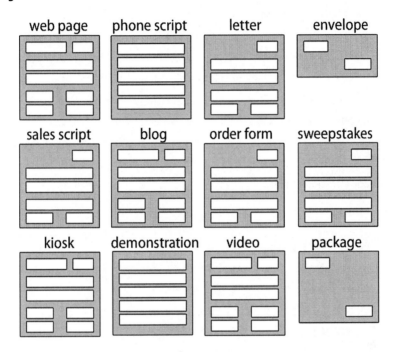

Figure 2.1 represents a small sample of obvious customer contacts. Notice that each contact is divided into sections (slots) representing message blocks that can be customized and personalized. Modern technology, digitized content, Internet-connected media, and advanced analytic methods can be used to determine what message fills each slot in each contact. These can be based on the customer, the time and location of the contact, inventory levels, news announcements, the customer's messaging device, or the goals and objectives of your company.

There are virtually limitless combinations of messages that can be delivered individually to each customer through each slot in each contact. Your company has no choice but to pay for each contact, so each slot in each contact should be treated as an asset. Customers also invest their time and money in each contact, ultimately, buying or not buying from you.

Slot is the container that presents a message to a customer during a contact. Slots exist within systems: they are variable text messages on a utility bill, shelf locations within a retail store, ad locations within a Web page, and personalized paragraphs within a telemarketing script. A system may present multiple slots during a given contact. Each slot can be given an estimated value, which is the expected return from presenting the best available message during a given interaction. In other words, **the monetization of contacts—the core concept of CxC Matrix—is implemented through the monetization of slots.**

Technology and business practices have evolved to enable your business to compete at this nano level. Every sub-message or "slot" in every contact represents the new competitive frontier—from the greeting on a voice mail, to each of 20 individual slots or sections in a single web page, to the labels on the outside of a package and the text message that appears on a customer's Personal Digital Assistant (PDA) as he enters your location.

Visualizing, analyzing, monetizing, and optimizing each slot in each contact is the foundation of the CxC Matrix. It assesses the effectiveness of each slot and each contact and provides companies and customers a platform to continuously innovate and improve the customer experience.

Single channel excellence: Amazon

Amazon, an ecommerce pioneer, expertly uses every square inch of a customer's screen to deliver a mosaic of offers and messages designed to stimulate interest, win more customer time, and generate additional revenue.

Look at the Amazon web page (Figure 2.2) and notice how Amazon uses

64 slots on the first page of its 14-1/2 pages about the featured book, *The Essential Drucker.*

It is obvious to advanced marketing practitioners and ecommerce professionals that Amazon has monetized each slot similarly to the way Google and DoubleClick monetize, barter, select, and continuously test, monitor, and report on the success of electronic ad placements. Amazon has spent millions on designing this page for this moment and for this customer, leveraging the knowledge it has collected from every similar search and web navigation route.

Figure 2.2 Amazon Slot Chart

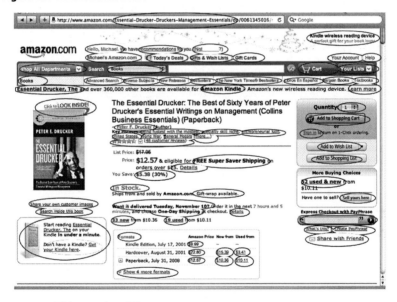

Web page slots: 263+

Each message is precisely determined, scripted, presented, arranged, ordered, and prioritized based on its probability to drive more revenue and harvest customer value.

When the customer clicks through to order the book, another stream of messages and offers appear in carefully arranged slots designed to secure the sale, up-sell services with format and packaging options, cross-sell additional items, and invite participation through referrals and reviews. When the book arrives, it is accompanied by a cost-justified set of fliers and promotions. Nothing is left to chance. No slot is wasted.

So, how does Amazon's 263+ advertising messages per web page make the customer feel? Was the customer also bombarded by additional messages while online. Was music playing? Was the TV on? Was the customer in a web café at the time? Was the customer simultaneously conducting business with your company?

This is just a small sample of the new marketing reality in which customers are exposed to tens of thousands of messages every week. They are approached through 20 to 100 entertainment and news channels, smart appliances, radio, billboards, signage, newspapers, magazines, product placements in shows and movies, Bluetooth-connected everything, RFID, and on and on. Channels are exploding, and customers are stuck in the middle of a mash-up of messages, promises, and offers.

You are not Amazon, and Amazon does not have all the answers

While Amazon's web page is a good example of monetizing every slot to achieve the best outcome per customer, Amazon chooses to compete only in online shopping. There is no phone number to call for shopping assistance or to order the Drucker book by phone. Go to the order page, and you will still find no phone number or online chat information. Amazon is smart enough to know that any phone or chat contact detracts from customer profit. Add a $10,000 television and stereo to your shopping cart, and you still have no phone numbers.

If you take the time to gather information about Amazon business programs, such as "Selling on Amazon," "Developer Services," or "Build an eCommerce Website," you will find no phone numbers. As elsewhere on the Internet, finding a phone number is a frustrating scavenger hunt, but Amazon knows that. It understands the value and costs associated with each contact.

Amazon's lesson

The Amazon example is a best practice for online shopping, but it is an inferior example for luxury shopping, in-person shopping, or direct TV and online shopping through QVC and home shopping networks. So experiment and test innovations, but be true to your core value proposition and manage your costs. Focus is key.

Similarly, business services solutions provided by Amazon online appear to be mostly self-service, even though most businesses pay a premium for hand-holding, expert advice, and face-to-face consultations.

The Amazon web page is used as an example because it is a graphic composite of offers strategically designed to continuously learn about the customer and grow revenue. The Amazon site clearly exemplifies how the stages of the consumer cycle, interests, and attributes are used to dynamically script each customer's experience.

This portion of Amazon's strategy and supporting technologies like Amazon's databases, algorithms, content management systems, and decision engines are the foundations for the next generation of marketing and managing customer contacts.

You, too, can Think Like a Customer

There are lots of strategies that Amazon uses that won't work for your company, but the CxC Matrix will help you identify simple improvements that reduce costs in weeks, not months, using a simple metric: yield per customer.

You'll quickly uncover untapped revenue and margin growth opportunities by tracing customer activities and exposing underused customer contacts.

The Matrix exposes underused contacts not only to internal departments and managers but also to selected third parties and partners. Allowing third parties to participate in company contacts by activities such as selling advertising space on a website, re-marketing alternative offers to internally low-potential customers, or including paid inserts in shipping cartons may generate incremental income at little or no cost.

From contact cacophony to clarity

Building a complete picture of every customer contact across your company and across every channel is not easy, and it won't be done overnight, but it is vital to aligning company resources to achieve optimum customer yield.

Whereas some companies want to *reduce* the number of their customer contacts and channels as costs per contact escalate, others want to *grow* the frequency and breadth of customer contacts in order to extract more value per customer, promote more products, get closer to customers, and generate referrals and affiliate revenue.

Easy to get started

Every customer contact has a cost, whether it is an email offer, an in-store salesperson, an information phone call, or a receipt handed to a customer. The CxC Matrix starts as a simple tool for companies to inventory and categorize every possible customer contact from the time a customer first becomes aware of a company or its products and services, through the buying decision, support services, and the time that the customer disposes of the product. Then, each contact is assigned an owner responsible for operation, technology, and execution. Each contact point or Matrix cell is measured for the number of customers who pass through it. Contacts are monetized to expose their cost and potential revenue and analyzed further to uncover revenue enhancement and cost savings contact-by-contact.

Corporate objectives executed per contact

A core CxC Matrix concept is that each customer contact can be managed according to your company's business objectives. The Matrix assumes that each contact can be handled more intelligently and that your company, customers, and a network of service and goods providers will participate in each customer contact.

The Matrix establishes "customer" as a corporate performance metric that spans and connects all departments, disciplines, systems, and processes.

Analyze the potential personalized treatments

The wealth of company and business knowledge, combined with knowledge of your customers, allows you to script the perfect customer interaction with a beginning, middle, and end, while assessing the customer's needs, values, and preferences. This accomplishes your company's current priorities and objectives. A high-tech example from Amazon was presented above. It's a sophisticated web page that presents and arranges multiple messages that can be configured and personalized for each customer. These messages are synthesized and synchronized through combinations of behavioral information, business rules, and service provider capabilities.

Continuous learning through data capture and behavior monitoring

The CxC Matrix provides an orderly method for capturing information from every contact and allows that information to be linked to performance by contact, channel, and department. The Matrix shows the comprehensive picture of how many customers are in each stage and channel and forecasts how many customers will move to which channels in which timeframes. The customers who don't move in the expected period of time are then available for closer inspection and analysis. For example, if you know that 100 people came into a store in an hour, 50 of them asked a sales associate a question, but only 2 actually made a purchase, you know you need to drill down to find out more about the customer experience of the 50 people who just wandered into the store and wandered out again, as well as the 48 who talked with a sales associate but didn't make a purchase.

The Matrix helps your company shorten its reaction time to market shifts and abrupt changes in customer preferences and behaviors, providing service flexibility and market nimbleness for an unprecedented competitive advantage.

The Matrix shepherds customers through the consumer cycle

Using the Matrix you can ensure that customers do not fall through the cracks in internal processes due to incomplete, fragmented, and disparate systems and missed intradepartmental hand-offs. The CxC Matrix provides a conceptual map of how customers meet their own needs by searching, finding, buying, and using products and services.

Because the CxC Matrix tracks all customer contacts and all customer experience threads, you can anticipate where your customers' next series of contacts are likely to occur, the channels they are likely to use, and even estimate the likely timing of the subsequent contacts.

"Nearly 60% of customers want you to let them begin an order in one channel (say, your website) and finish it in another (say, your downtown store.) By 2012, these types of cross-channel transactions could account for 38% of all retail sales."

—"Strategies for Satisfying the Spoiled Consumer with Cross-Channel Execution," June 2008 webinar promotion, *Multichannel Merchant*

Think Like a Customer

Even in its simplest form, the CxC Matrix provides a platform for interdepartmental dialogue and solution-building. Managers and employees "get it." They can see that there is a marketing role in every customer contact. Discussing business challenges and opportunities using the customer as a vehicle makes obvious sense: it improves operations and quality for the customer, and measures performance by customer. Employees from all levels are empowered to participate as they speak on the customer's behalf, and they can easily chart a customer's current and potential paths through the company.

The mantra "Think Like a Customer!" opens conversations to innovative solutions, exposes artifacts of corporate folklore and management blind spots, all centered around and measured by customer flow and contact performance.

The CxC Matrix is common sense to business improvement

Like everyone else, I have been the customer of countless companies that have left money on the table; that failed to fully use my time and investment in learning their processes and operations; that failed to simply ask for more business, or failed to make me aware of how I could better use their services. This is what the Matrix exposes—the opportunity in each instance, interaction, and contact. The Matrix seeks to generate additional revenue streams from every single contact, customer-by-customer.

The Matrix leverages existing resources

Most companies already possess all of the ingredients required to achieve tremendous success. All that is required is some level of process redesign, repurposing current capabilities and resources, modifying current operating practices, and expanding often-unused functionality in current systems.

A large amount of value is uncovered when your managers simply visualize their business in the Matrix. Visualization reveals what management and employees intrinsically know:

- Customers get lost within the company's silos.

- Missed departmental, process, and systems hand-offs forfeit opportunities and increase costs.

- Analyzing business from the customer's perspective unveils opportunities and risks.

The Matrix clearly depicts what you already know—that your company could perform better if only you:

- Knew about all of the customer's activities.

- Were able to leverage all of the options at each consumer cycle when *you* answer the phone or greet a customer in person.

- Were able to leverage all of the options when the customer logs in to a web page or sits alone at a desk and opens a package.

These contacts are rich with untapped, unmeasured opportunities, and the Matrix encourages and enables companies to tap into underperforming assets.

Why now? Managing at the contact level is a capability made possible through technical advances that standardize data access through open systems. These systems engage customers via the Internet and through Internet-connected devices, services, and communities. However, because many companies operate in silos, and marketing managers are not familiar with the capabilities of the new technology and may not speak the same language as the information technology department, much of the capability of the systems goes unused.

Think about it. Traditionally billing statements were static pieces of paper that listed items and cost. But with digitization and customer database connectivity, you can leverage the customer's invoice to present new product offers, stuff the billing statement envelope with targeted messages, and promote a new service on the outside of the envelope in one, albeit complex, contact.

Electronic billing statements afford even greater flexibility and personalization. They can be accessed and delivered across any electronic network and formatted to each customer's specifications. They can include Internet web page links to product, service, warranty, maintenance, and corporate information. They can spawn alerts and other activities.

The customer billing statement, historically viewed as an operations and finance department basic requirement and cost of doing business, can now also be viewed as a marketing tool and valued by the amount of potential incremental revenue it generates. It can notify customers, generate referrals and revenue from third parties that pay for this specific customer's attention in this contact.

Every contact is rich with revenue potential and cost savings when exposed through the Matrix. Hundreds of similar opportunities exist throughout your customer contact network. This is the domain and the function of the CxC Matrix.

The alternative to contact chaos

The purpose of the Matrix is to remove the chaos and enable the transparency of every customer contact so that marketers can be in control and leverage every internal and external resource.

Per-contact costs such as telephone support minutes, envelopes, and emails seem to be tightly managed to peak efficiency, yet cost per customer continues to increase due to escalating messages, offers, services, and product complexity. This complexity also appears to be the source of customer dissatisfaction and disengagement.

The burden of creating, responding to, managing, and monitoring customer messages overwhelms companies. Costs continue to escalate while communications quality, management oversight, governance, and controls affect fewer than one-third of contacts. In-bound voice messages, emails, letters, ever-expanding web mentions, customer reviews, chat sessions, YouTube videos, customer-generated media, partner communications, and all of the person-to-person service calls and sales pitches continue to grow out of control, raising costs and business risk exposure across multiple departments and multiple fronts.

Today, public relations is at a tremendous disadvantage when injured, disgruntled, and scorned customers can cheaply and easily post a message on an electronic bulletin board, blog, or chat room, send an email to a news service, or post a video on YouTube. How does a company respond? Protecting your brands and your company against risk is another area managed through the Matrix. In bygone times, headquarters' executives sometimes did not know about a customer issue or crisis until they read about it in the newspaper.

The CxC Matrix brings order to the chaos of the out-of-control customer contact system and provides a means to manage, observe, measure, and monitor customer contacts.

Five essential Matrix deliverables

The Matrix provides ease of use with these five steps:

Visualize: The Matrix emphasizes visualization to provide the broadest understanding of customers across departments and functions and among partner companies.

Analyze: The Matrix provides a rich data set for companies to analyze performance by contact, by customer, and in conjunction with existing metrics.

Monetize: Every business decision and every scenario—complete with visibility of its downstream and upstream impact—is monetized in the Matrix.

Prioritize: Focus time, resources, and effort on the contact areas that show the greatest potential return. Automate what works, and invest your resources in innovation.

Optimize: The Matrix provides a means to quantify, replicate, and automate best practices, leveraging its analytical and monetization foundation to fuel continuous improvement.

Isn't this just sales and marketing?

If marketing is responsible for generating more revenue from every customer, answering every phone, designing every product, selecting every office location, and shaking every customer's hand, then yes—the Matrix is just marketing.

While the CxC Matrix focuses on customers and contacts, the traditional domain and function of marketing, most of the contacts (especially underused contacts) are not advertisements and sales contacts. They are contacts across the entire consumer cycle and all its stages and throughout every channel.

Let's find out more about the Matrix and how to implement it in your company.

CHAPTER 3

Think Like a Customer!
The Customer's Version of the Story

Understanding business contact-by-contact, customer-by-customer

Figure 3.1

Remember, the customer process is the most important process in every business. **The most important!**

Need, Shop, Buy

When you think like a customer, you get a simple picture of your business. Or more accurately, you get a simple picture of how customers describe your business in their context and from memory. Describing a business from the customer's perspective exposes where and how customers navigate their purchase decisions, their decision paths, and the options they select and deselect in each contact.

We will use these three simple customer process steps in buying a lawn mower to illustrate how the CxC Matrix works: Need, Shop, Buy. Replace "lawn mower" with "main frame computer" or "insurance" if you want to simulate a business-to-business transaction. The design accommodates nearly any product or service.

In the Customer's words:

I received an email from my local hardware store that had a picture of a lawn mower similar to the one I had bought three years ago.

I clicked on the picture and saw a good price, with a trade-in for my current lawn mower. So, I drove over to the hardware store and bought the new mower.

They delivered it and picked up the old one the same day.

Figure 3.2

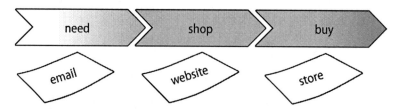

The simple need, shop, buy scenario gets a little more complicated when we expose the actual contacts that took place between the customer and the business and resulted in the customer's purchase.

Note that the customer recounts each contact in sequence and notes the channel (email, website, store, or home). Presented this simply, it is reasonable to assume that anyone at your company or even your competitors could understand the steps in the customer's process.

However, as with many illustrative business scenarios, the simple process does not adequately convey the amount of design, planning, and coordinated execution required across the company to make the customer's purchase seem "uneventful."

Unfortunately, processes like these are often created through trial and error. As a result, your company and customers may suffer through a number of mismanaged contacts, broken processes, and missed hand-offs before you fine-tune the process and deliver the best outcome.

To highlight the simple elegance of the lawn mower story, look at the diagram below for a sample of the potential problems that could have happened at each contact:

Figure 3.3

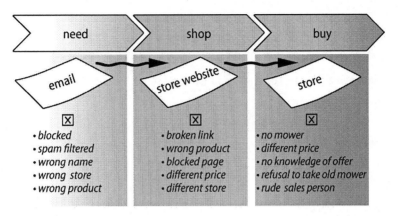

The potential negative outcomes highlighted in Figure 3.3 include a couple of points worth mentioning:

- The email, website, and store contacts bear a cost, whether successful or not.

- Contact costs are not funded until the mower purchase.

- Each contact's success is dependent on the success of the upstream and downstream contacts.

- To succeed, each contact requires synchronization across marketing, operations, sales, fulfillment, website, store, finance, reverse logistics, legal, and partners.

- Failure at any of the contacts, malfunction, or defect in execution raises costs and endangers the revenue objective of the business.

- Each contact contains substantial data that, when put in the customer's context, delineates the success of the business.

Trial and error is expensive for both your company and customers, wasting internal resources and your customers' time while foregoing eventual revenue. The Matrix provides a means for you to plot each of these contacts and to observe the potential gaps in communications, connectivity, and operational processes. It allows you to minimize errors while ensuring a positive customer outcome.

The Matrix also captures the success rate of all customers going through each contact or process stage. The number of customers who survive from "need" to "shop" to "buy" is the measurement of success at each contact. By exposing each contact, the elements of each contact, and the resources accountable for each contact, you can assess performance and modify the process to improve the outcome.

The Matrix captures and codifies the company's most successful contact paths, enabling replication and continuous improvement for future promotions. Collectively, the repository of best practices, promotions, marketing, sales, operations, and customer-service contact processes becomes the company's unique knowledge base for success.

Now . . . for the rest of the story

While the customer relayed his journey, which led to happily mowing his lawn, he did not acknowledge, remember, or recognize the other contacts the business used to ultimately secure his mower purchase. He was bombarded with messages attempting to get his attention, to prompt and prod him into "needing" a new mower. Some of the additional contacts are outlined in Figure 3.4.

Figure 3.4

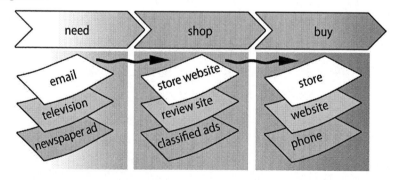

Once the customer engaged in the initial contact, each subsequent contact was carefully choreographed with a single objective: to create the urgency to replace his three-year-old mower.

Part of the well-executed design entailed educating the customer on "how to buy a mower" and specifically, "how easy it is to buy from Acme." Additionally, each contact carefully persuaded him that "Acme Local Hardware is your best choice for garden equipment." Every contact and sub-message in every contact was aimed at these two objectives.

Choreographing each step in a consumer cycle

The seemingly simple customer "need" was the result of multiple efforts coordinated across marketing, advertising, product sponsors and co-op advertising partners. Each group's efforts focused on getting the customer's attention, building his awareness of his need for a lawn mower, and convincing him that now was the best time to act. All of the messages were coordinated to reinforce the value of a new mower and to create urgency to "act now!"

The "shop" step fulfilled the customer's need for more information to make his purchase. Each contact was designed to reinforce the superior benefits the customer would achieve by upgrading his mowing experience, providing details and specifications that were carefully presented and packaged to meet his specific needs and preferences.

The customer's needs and interests were distilled from:

- His previous mower purchase,
- Subsequent store purchases,
- Web page downloads,
- Local market information,
- Purchased third party lifestyle and interests data, including:
  - The types of lawn products the customer purchased,
  - The price point at which the customer purchased,
  - The total amount of outdoor home expenditures the customer made over the past three years,
  - Other information not directly related to home and hardware purchases.

All of this information was used to build a company memory that mirrors what a top sales and customer relationship manager would remember and use to persuade a customer to "buy." The company invested in technology, data, and training with the Chief Executive Officer's mandate to become each targeted customer's "single, most trusted, most knowledgeable source."

Same customer outcome, low tech delivery

Would the customer know the difference between this highly technical, tightly orchestrated, overly complex sales, marketing, and operations process versus receiving a chance email from the salesperson who sold him his old mower three years ago?

No, and it makes no difference. Either way, the customer buys the mower.

What the CxC Matrix provides your business, regardless of its size and infrastructure, is a means to delineate the best way to manage individual contacts by matching your business objectives with the customer's values and preferences.

The company's side of the story—orchestrating the contacts

Dissecting the mower contacts

Each customer contact contains multiple messages. Figure 3.5 exposes the 47 message slots used in the simplified need, shop, buy story. Each slot can hold a message, an offer, instructions, contact information, third party advertisements, images, operational information, news, or government warnings. It is constrained only by limitations in the medium, data, technology, or ability to personalize. Without limitations, messages can vary by individual, location, time of day, product inventory, and so forth. Just about any attribute can be used to prescribe the message, wording, images, colors, or order language for each individual slot.

Figure 3.5

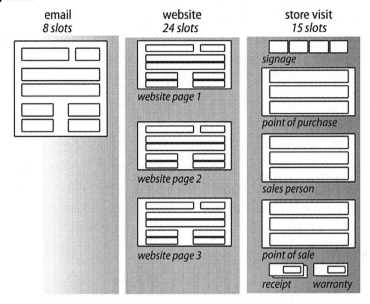

Here's how we count the slots:

- Email: 8 slots—banner, offer, closing, contact information, return-address message, right border, header, footer;

- Web page: 24 slots—3 pages, 8 slots per page;

- Store visit: signs—4 slots; point of purchase—3 slots (display literature and rack); sales person—3 slots (greeting, information extend, close); point of sale—3 slots; receipt—2 slots (back and front); warranty card—1 slot.

There are numerous additional slots at the store and throughout this customer's process.

Digital printing, digital technologies, and Internet-connected devices such as kiosks, websites, and point-of-purchase displays are equipped to deliver multi-part messages and groups of messages as directed by a set of rules based on customer type, location, customer segment, time of day, or any other set of rules.

Each contact is a container for slots

Definition: A container is the specific contact point within a channel. Containers distinguish the individual contacts within a contact. The nature and attributes of a container depend on the channel or medium. A container can be the greeting in an in-person sales call, a brochure, an FAQ on a web page. Containers have specific dimensions. Retail stores are containers with actual physical walls, shelves, brick, and mortar. Dealer or distributor containers may refer to separate businesses. Containers in an advertising channel may be different issues of a magazine or time slots purchased on different television stations. A web container may be a web page, while a call center container would be an individual telemarketing script.

Each of the three channels represented in Figure 3.5—email, website, and store—has individual messaging capabilities. The channel's medium provides a set of capabilities and constraints, as does the individual contact point. For example, the signs in the store are not likely to vary to present a different message for each customer, whereas email does provide individualized messaging. Similarly, specifications for a web page will be quite different from store receipt container specifications. The web page contains 7 more slots for messages. It also accommodates images and provides much more space per slot for messages. The receipt is restricted to one message on each side printed in black and white and the message cannot exceed 144 characters.

Key takeaway: Inventorying each medium's specifications and slots enables companies to manage slots across the company from a single system.

Too much to measure

With so many messages, tracking which slot and message combination "works" becomes nearly impossible. However, assembling all of the contacts and their components in the sequence, environment, and context that the customer experiences is essential to understanding each element's performance, as well as identifying and codifying success. With this understanding we are not only able to better measure performance but we are also able to predict the outcome and likely success of similar initiatives delivered to similar customers.

For example, the mower story's success comes not just from the customer's click on the picture of the mower in the email. It also comes from the email's subject line, the offers and messages contained in the email, and all of the messages that preceded and succeeded each contact. The Matrix uniquely measures not only what "works" but also measures the absence of activity related to other messages and contacts. The mower offer may have successfully worked in this sequence because it was positioned next to a more expensive alternative or in a sequence of other customer activities.

The CxC Matrix is designed to conceptually represent the multitude of variations across the customer's contact path while capturing the peripheral messages and contact elements, giving you the most comprehensive view of all customer contact experiences, successful and unsuccessful. The Matrix enables scenario building and experimentation providing a platform for customer-partnered innovation.

All of these elements can be individually measured, as well as in combination with others using the CxC Matrix, to assess the investment of each department and the company's total investment per customer, per program, per channel, per contact, and per message.

The loudest sound in business is customer silence

We can easily see how the Matrix measures contacts and contact sequence, but the Matrix is equally powerful when used to measure what did not happen. Most business measurement systems count transactions, customers, inventory, but the CxC Matrix uniquely highlights the events that were expected in the customer sequence, but did not happen. For example, the group of customers that research a product, conduct all of the pre-buying evaluation then do not buy. The customers that buy and pay for a product but do not register, install or use the product. The Matrix highlights changes in customer behavior and alerts managers to investigate further while also providing a rich data set to examine customer contact data. The Matrix uniquely measures when the voice of the customer goes silent.

Summary

Each contact and each message within each contact bears a cost as well as corresponding direct and potential revenues.

Each slot in each contact in each channel has its own value while a series of contacts and a series of slots presented to a customer reflect your company's total investment and return per customer.

The mix of contacts that engage a customer is the most underused asset at most companies. Extracting the optimum value contact-by-contact has always been feasible for very small companies communicating through limited channels to a small number of customers. However, using the Matrix and leveraging advances in technology, analytics, and process design, all companies can compete contact-by-contact.

CHAPTER 4

Capturing the Customer Experience

The value of a business is the value of its customer contacts. The CxC Matrix enables your company, customers, and all stakeholders to visualize, monetize, analyze, and optimize customers contact-by-contact.

The Matrix's primary purpose is to help you align your corporate objectives with the customer's values and preferences at each contact. This approach leverages current technological capabilities, while also serving as a framework for upcoming and future customer and business technologies.

The CxC Matrix provides a detailed framework to classify and manage customer contacts. It places every potential customer contact with a company—the company's brand, products, and services—into the intersection of the consumer cycle and company's channels. Channels are the physical, digital, and virtual locations where customer contacts occur.

CxC Matrix Customer Stages

Matrix stages represent the customer's journey to satisfy a need or want for a product or service in the course of the relationship or transaction. They are the horizontal dimension of a CxC Matrix.

The following are the stages in the customer's journey.

Figure 4.1

1. Awareness	2. Information	3. Identification	4. Selection	5. Negotiation	6. Contract	7. Logistics	8. Delivery	9. Acceptance	10. $ Collection	11. Use	12. Care/Support	13. Repair	14. Disposal	15. Community
Need			Shop			Buy				Use				

Need

1. Customer becomes aware of a need.

2. Customer begins preliminary research of how to satisfy need.

3. Customer begins to qualify solutions, vendors, approaches as either "in" or "out."

Shop

4. Customer examines offers from providers considering specific product and service attributes (ingredients, warranty, availability, total cost of operation).

5. Customer prepares for purchase, weighing perceived value and benefits of selection against his own value set, options, and alternatives such as delay, buy used, no purchase, upgrade, and optional add-ons.

6. Customer and company contract to provide service and/or product, agree on price, payment, delivery, warranty, etc.

Buy

7. Customer and company agree on product and service fulfillment terms —take now, send to location, immediate delivery, multi-point delivery, multi-user subscription, and conditional incremental delivery.

8. Customer receives product or initiates service.

9. Customer accepts product as delivered, unwraps and assembles, and initiates service.

10. Customer pays, including the entire payment and financing process: down payments, partial payments, incremental and subscription-based payments, and all exchanges of funds and fund equivalents.

Use

11. Ongoing and one-time customer use, including passive use of a product or service that a customer may not knowingly consume, such as life insurance, product and service warranties, and product possession, and storage.

12. From box opening and assembly instructions through operation and maintenance guidelines, "How to contact us" messages, and all contacts related to assistance in using and maintaining products and services.

13. Contact resulting from malfunctioning or perceived malfunctioning of product or service, from unexpected or unplanned use, or from another situation involving the product.

14. Contacts related to the product and service's end life, requiring physical disposal, service secession acknowledgment, expiration notice and related activities, re-selling and recycling, and replenishment, including selling and re-selling the product. Also includes product and service purchase and use artifacts, such as bills, receipts, usage summary logs, archived information, product, and service liability contacts.

15. Interactions related to customer word-of-mouth, social networking, review and recommendation platforms, community market sites such as Craigslist, Facebook, LinkedIn, Amazon, Froogle, eBay, etc., membership clubs and groups, trade and after-market organizations, collectors' clubs, regulatory bodies, trade publications, websites, web forums, blogs, social networking, and product reviews.

The CxC Matrix stages address the process design issues that you must deal with in assembling a cohesive, high-quality, end-to-end customer experience. It also recognizes that each stage may be handled by different departments or even different companies.

CxC Matrix channel categories

This level CxC Matrix classifies channels into six categories, grouping them from the customer's perspective and representing the customer's expectations for service, intimacy, and urgency, including Geography, Digital, Location, Third Party, One-on-One, and Community, shown in Figure 4.2.

Figure 4.2 CxC Matrix

	1. Awareness	2. Information	3. Identification	4. Selection	5. Negotiation	6. Contract	7. Logistics	8. Delivery	9. Acceptance	10. $ Collection	11. Use	12. Care/Support	13. Repair	14. Disposal	15. Community
Geography	X	X													X
Digital	X	X	X	X	X							X			X
Location	X	X	X	X	X	X	X				X	X			X
Third party	X	X	X	X											X
One-on-one	X	X	X					X	X		X	X			
Community		X	X									X			X

Plotting "The Mower Story" for the single customer told from the company's perspective depicts the total contacts made across all channels and the resulting revenue achieved at Stage 6: Contract. Each cell in the summarized Matrix above represents a contact or set of contacts grouped by the type of channel.

Contacts are recorded in CRM systems, web log files, marketing systems, financial transaction systems, call center and telemarketing systems, contact management, sales management, advertising tracking systems, customer registration systems, loyalty club, membership and affiliate systems and any number of internal and third party formal and informal, paper and electronic data capture systems.

The importance of visualization

Before you can affect customer performance, your company must collectively understand its customers' experiences. The Matrix provides a mental model of customer situations for the purposes of making rapid and appropriate decisions at each contact, as shown in Figure 4.3.

Figure 4.3 CxC Matrix: Customer Mapping

CUSTOMER LIFE STAGE

CHANNEL	Awareness	Selection	Purchase	Use	Support	Repair	Dispose
Dealer	X	X	X			X	X
Retail						X	X
Events	X	X					
Field sales							
Call center		X		X	X		
Web	X	X	X	X	X		
Email	X		X	X	X		
Direct mail	X						
Magazine	X						
Newspaper	X						
Radio							
TV	X						
Outdoor	X						
Community	X	X			X	X	X

The picture is important: More than half the brain is devoted to processing visuals. As much as 80 percent of our learning is visually oriented.

Customer Mapping—follow the customer

The customer flow diagram (Figure 4.3) is an excellent tool for examining cause-and-effect relationships across various customer experience scenarios. These diagrams reveal patterns and changes in patterns that may expose competitive threats, market changes, or product and service issues, among other things. The diagram can also be used to strategize and design responses to various strategic scenarios: ending a product line; alternative distribution channel; launching a new channel; charging for previously free services; partnership and outsourcing options.

These visualizations, or customer experience maps, help all departments and experts gain better customer understanding. They often uncover why certain customer policies, communication programs, pricing programs, and delivery programs do not work or are poorly received by customers. Take a simple logistics problem such as when a customer submits a large multi-product order and requires pieces to be delivered to multiple locations. The Matrix can be used to map the best customer outcome at each location and in each contact based on corporate objectives and individual endpoint potential. This scenario seems simple to the parties intimately involved in the customer's operations on a day-to-day basis, but it may be conceptually incomprehensible to a new person in the finance department or in shipping who has to contact "the customer" about a delay in shipping on one item. Who do you call?

To simplify, individual channels can be grouped into the following types:

Geography

- TV
- Community events
- Radio
- Billboards
- Outdoor
- Signage
- Magazines

Digital

- Banner ads
- Website
- Company email
- Blast email
- Webinars
- On-line demonstrations
- Hosted & sponsored online content, video, etc.
- Campaign management email
- Support email
- Click for chat

Location

- Store
- In-store promotions
- Demonstrations

Third Party

- Package inserts
- Private-label partners
- Affiliate offers
- Advertorials
- Resellers
- Paid analysts

- Paid reviewers
- Aggregators
- Brokers
- Distributors
- Non-captive sales agents
- Paid subject matter experts

One-on-One

- Inbound telemarketing
- Online customer support
- Text Messaging, SMS
- Email
- Hosted, sponsored contests
- Email billing statements
- Shipments
- Catalog
- Customer service
- Statement inserts
- Service click for chat
- Direct mail
- Outbound telemarketing in person sales call

Community

- Independent membership organizations
- Clubs
- Social networks
- Subject matter experts
- Reviewers
- Independent trade organizations
- Blogosphere
- Trade shows
- Public relations
- Press/trade magazines

Figure 4.4   CxC Matrix

		1. Awareness	2. Information	3. Identification	4. Selection	5. Negotiation	6. Contract	7. Logistics	8. Delivery	9. Acceptance	10. $ Collection	11. Use	12. Care & Support	13. Repair	14. Dispose	15. Community
Geography	TV															
	Events															
	Radio															
	Outdoor															
	Signage															
	Magazines															
Digital	Banner ads															
	Website															
	Company email															
	Campaign management email															
	Support email															
	Sales click for chat															
Location	In-store promotions															
	Kiosks															
Third party	Package inserts															
	Private-label partners															
	Affiliate offers															
One-on-one	Inbound telemartketing															
	Online customer support															
	Billing statements															
	Shipments															
	Door-to-door															
	Catalog															
	Customer service															
	Statement inserts															
	Service click for chat															
	Direct mail															
	Outbound telemartketing															
Community	Press/trade magazines															
	Blogs															

You should list every channel and medium to create a comprehensive list of all customer contacts, not just the channels you currently use but all channels available to the consumer, your partners, and communities. Further detail can be added to deepen insights and choreograph the messages and treatments in each experience stage.

Marketing, communication, and customer-service managers find this level of detail useful for planning campaigns, alerting departments about the impact of upcoming programs, and preparing downstream channels for increases or decreases in customer flow.

A chart like Figure 4.4 can also be used to show the cost and benefit of each contact and each cell's success rate in moving customers to the contract stage.

Think Like a Customer!
Customer Flow Through the CxC Matrix

Visualizing the "mower" customer's life stages and customer-experience history helps every person involved in brainstorming, designing, executing, and measuring the "buy a mower" program. Stakeholders can quickly assess their role in the program, as well as the customer's progress and the program's and your company's objectives.

Broadening our view of the customer's experience to not just the purchase but his use of the product, repairs, and eventual disposal, we expose more marketing opportunities and the ability to realize greater revenue from this customer over the customer's entire lifetime.

The customer's perspective includes two lawn mowers—the one he purchased three years ago and the new mower that the customer "wanted" now through marketing persuasion. The contacts look like this:

Figure 4.5

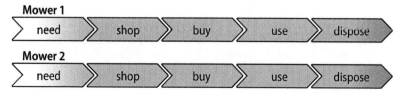

Key takeaway: The customer process is the same, but the difference over time is the customer's perspective, the company's message, execution capabilities, and offers.

In this hypothetical example, you can replace "mower" with a computer, car, consulting service, cell phone, or any other product or service. The customer process is standardized here for analysis and planning purposes.

Customers dictate the pace at which they move through their buying stages. Customers also dictate the agreement terms and conditions required to continue to conduct business. The cycle stops and the customer does not continue to the subsequent stage, or completely ceases all contacts when he decides your company's proposition or his experience with your company is no longer customer worthy.

You can attempt to accelerate "need" by growing the perceived value of buying, switching, upgrading, and converting, but the ultimate success comes down to successfully aligning corporate objectives (sell more product X at Y margin over the next 30 days) to the customer's need (customer needs product X). This is easily tested by asking the simple question, "Is our proposition customer worthy?" Ultimately, the customer decides.

Visualization clears up what may appear to be data anomalies or errors when business and marketing analysts examine program performance, financial implications, and operational design. Using the hypothetical scenario as an example, it is simple and logical to treat the "Mower 2" contacts and customer life cycle as sequential events as presented in the simple Matrix view. Here is a visual depiction of this mistake:

Figure 4.6

Mower 1   Mower 2

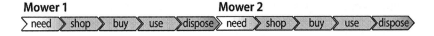

In reality, the customer life stages often overlap (and occur in varying sequences) when buying a new product or service. For a period of time, the customer has two similar products, two service providers, or two instances of a software solution that they are maintaining.

The customer's actual sequence looked more like this:

Figure 4.7

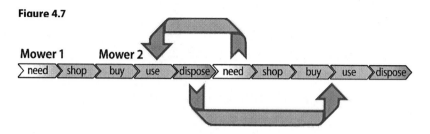

Lawn Mower 1 and Mower 2 coexisted for a while, and the time overlap may have caused issues for the company, including incompatible functionality, confusion in support areas, registration, support, and warranty and exchange mistakes. The Matrix can also depict the downstream impact of the customer's decision to keep the old mower and return the new mower. This degree of transparency about the customer's actions can shed light on operational issues and opportunities, customer service challenges, campaign results, sales efforts, and fraud.

Advanced CxC Matrix concepts

A customer's experiences with your company are often more complex than the simple, one-dimensional presentation we use in this book can express. The visual representations used throughout this book are used to simply convey the CxC Matrix's underlying concepts and mathematical formulas used to measure, manage and predict the outcome of multi-party, multi-channel, dynamic customer relationships. In practice, customers may have multiple experiences with a brand and with your company, whether buying multiple products over time or multiple products and services purchased to meet a single need.

The simple sequence depicted here does not always appear to happen in order, stages may be repeated, stalled and restarted, and stages may occur outside a company's direct view.

As a result, customers may have multiple simultaneous experiences, which may or may not impact each other. A contact with a member of a customer's family or an employee of a large customer may be mishandled and threaten apparently unrelated customer potential value. The Matrix enables managers to isolate illogical flows, events and consequences for further investigation and repair. Linking together all of a customer's experiences can show how a bad experience or a poor contact can negatively impact other seemingly unrelated experiences, like order cancellations or a customer's request to receive a single shipment of multiple items.

Figure 4.8 provides a conceptual view of the interrelationship of multiple customer experiences at a corporate level down to a business, product, and marketing level. This type of analysis shows how you can extend product lines or your brand by understanding how customers value and recognize the brand when making purchasing decisions.

Figure 4.8 Corporate Customer Experience Roll-up

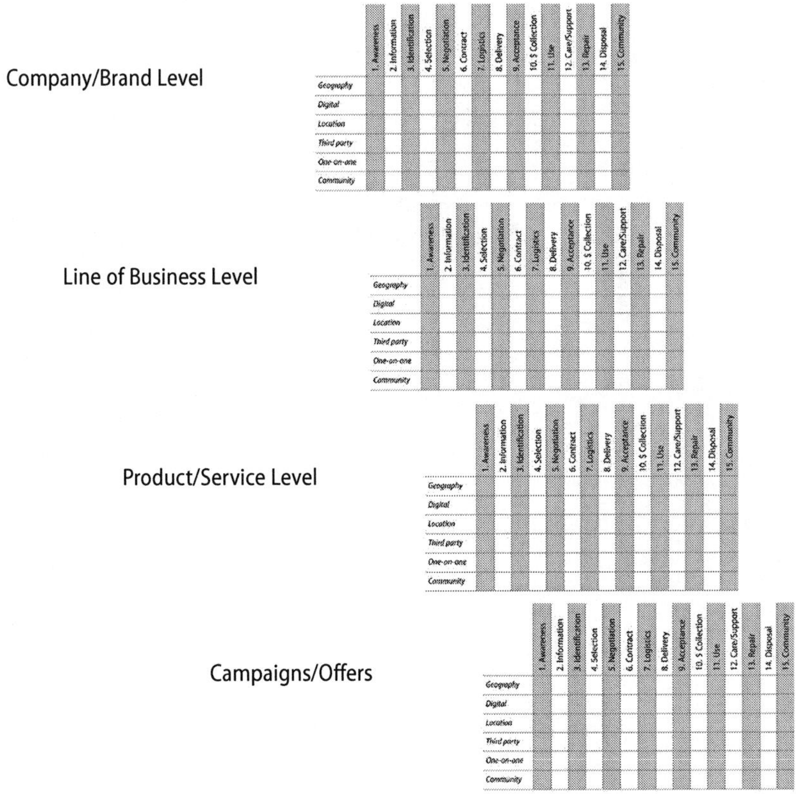

Figure 4.8 is just one of several drill-down or hierarchical CxC Matrix views meant to depict how customers can:

- Have relationships and contacts with multiple areas in a company,
- Be involved in multiple programs,
- Be at various stages with different parts of a company or group of companies responsible for delivering a product or service.

The visual Matrix helps managers better understand the interrelationships and dependencies where performance and operations are linked to customers. This view of customer linkage also helps you better assess resource allocation and better leverage overlapping processes and resources. This process view unveils opportunities for resource consolidation, new delivery and support models, and new product and service innovations. Likewise, the customer-level view reduces double counting customer opportunities across divisions and product areas.

Figure 4.9 Multi-Customer Contact Roll Up

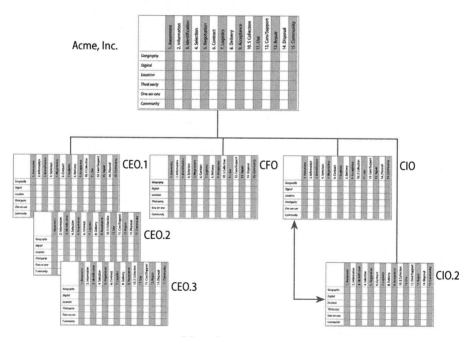

CIO vendor awareness through presentation triggers new company opportunity for unrelated service interest from same company spawns new experience *CIO.2.* New sale?

The CxC Matrix (Figure 4.9) depicts the common occurrence of multiple decision-makers from Acme, Inc. (customer) participating in one purchase consideration, where each contact, CEO, CFO and CIO has his or her own contact streams. In this case, the CEO is considering multiple services from this company represented as CEO.1, CEO.2, CEO.3.

It is very important that you identify all of the decisions-makers, their roles and collective contacts across the consumer lifecycle and ongoing throughout the customer's relationship.

In a business-to-consumer example, this concept may represent a husband, wife, and child looking to replace a family car or choose a college. The visual also shows how an experience can spawn and link another experience. For example, at the contract stage, the CIO was also introduced to a new hardware protection program that spawned an entirely new customer experience (CIO.2).

It is important to note that the individual experiences can be examined discreetly and at a rolled-up level in the Master CxC Matrix at the top.

CHAPTER 5

How Complicated Can One Click of a Mouse Be?

Aligning customer processes with company processes

In the previous chapters, we examined one customer's series of contacts across channels and media by stages in the consumer cycle. In this chapter, we walk through a customer experience, digging deeper into the company's contact management view, using the Matrix to connect the customer's journey to internal operations, systems, and department owners.

Again, we will start with the same lawn mower story from the customer's perspective and add detail using the CxC Matrix building blocks. This Matrix reduces the 15 stages of the consumer cycle to seven in order to make the example easier to follow.

Figure 5.1

CxC stage	Need		Shop		Buy		Use
	Awareness	Information	Selection	Negotiation	Contract	Logistics	Support
Customer view	receive email offer	search research	standard or deluxe	free for 90 days	terms & conditions	receive product	product query

Note: The CxC Matrix, which consists of 15 Customer Stages, is reduced here to seven to make the example easier to follow.

Consumer cycle and CxC Matrix stages combined

The Customer View

CxC Matrix Stage 1 *Awareness*

Customer awareness for need "new lawn mower" generated by email. By opening the email and clicking on the mower offer, the customer moves from the "Awareness Stage" to the "Information Stage." Marketing, advertising, and sales successfully persuaded the customer to gather information about fulfilling his need.

CxC Matrix Stage 2 *Information*

Customer opens promotional email, selects product, and is connected to promotion-specific "lawn mower" web page. Customer reads information, and clicks on links for more mower research. Additionally, the customer enters the product name, model number, and the word "reviews" into a Google search panel and begins reading review pages, expert comments, and user comments. The customer also contacts friends and neighbors about their lawn mower experiences.

CxC Matrix Stage 4 *Selection*

Customer refines mower needs and the features he wants based on information, value considerations, and his own circumstances in Matrix Stage 3, *Identification* (not shown). The customer then selects his preferred mower type, brand, and a set of potential vendors. He returns to the Acme Hardware Store website three more times in two days and visits the manufacturer's website four more times before confirming his selection.

CxC Matrix Stage 5 *Negotiation*

The customer clicks on the "add to cart" button on the website and fills in his information. He experiments by adding and removing mower add-on features and goes back and forth between model options. He looks for "free shipping" as he has seen from other online vendors, and he factors in assembly cost and time across each of his options. The customer abandons the "Acme Hardware Store" online shopping cart and heads to his local Acme Hardware Store with his email printed out and his web order page in hand. He also prints out competing offers from other vendors.

CxC Matrix Stage 6 *Contract*

The customer is greeted by a store salesman who takes him to the lawn mower section. The customer agrees to the price and the special offer to deliver the mower to his house and exchange his current mower. He pays by credit card at the register and receives a receipt that explains the store's return policy. It also offers extended warranty protection for purchases over $50.

CxC Matrix Stage 7 *Logistics*

The customer arranges for the mower to be delivered between 3:00 and 5:00 p.m. and agrees to have his current mower near his driveway for removal.

CxC Matrix Stage 12 *Support*

The customer mows his lawn for two weeks and notices a "funny" sound when the mower is shutting off. He both calls support and goes online to research his problem.

The CxC Matrix exposes some of the underpinnings of the company's success in selling the mower by exposing each contact from the company's perspective.

Figure 5.2 Think Like a Customer (TLC) Stage

CxC stage	Need		Shop		Buy		Use
	Awareness	Information	Selection	Negotiation	Contract	Logistics	Support
Customer view	receive email offer	search research	standard or deluxe	free for 90 days	terms & conditions	receive product	product query
Depart-ment	• marketing & ecommerce	• marketing web • PPC agency • product management • partners	• product management • ecommerce • operations • distribution	• product management • sales • finance	• sales • legal • finance	• operations • distribution • shipping • partner	• customer care • operations • training

The Department View

What appears to the customer as simply clicking on an email, selecting a couple of products, and hitting a "buy" button is a complex series of business rules, business arrangements, inter-company hand-offs, and information exchanges connecting a minimum of 8 departments and as many as 14 systems.

Figure 5.3 Department Responsibility And Accountability Metrics & KPIs

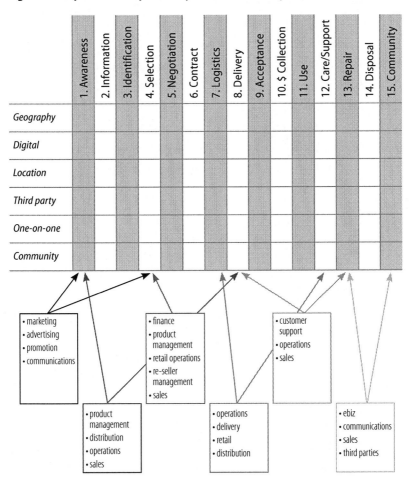

This example shows a bit of the complexity that occurs on the company side of this "simple" experience. The Department View often stirs discussions among department heads, line managers, and front-line personnel who relate vivid incidents of when the "simple" process went wrong.

After the finger-pointing and customer stories subside, individuals quickly begin to identify improvements, innovations, and alternative product and service configurations that can be deployed at little or no expense.

Employees are frequently surprised by how the Matrix connects departments and individuals across functions. The customer perspective connects the downstream and upstream impacts of each department's activities and decisions, expanding the employees' understanding of their roles in the customer process, while educating them about the rest of the company's operations.

This horizontal and departmental customer experience view is highly summarized and easy to create for your own business. I recommend walking through this exercise with representatives from these departments to provoke customer-centric discussions.

Department-to-Department Hand-offs

To ensure customer success, companies must capture and convey customer, offer, service, and message component information from department to department. The Department View exposes the departments and individuals responsible for each element of each contact; for creating messages; for delivering the messages; and all other activities related to ensuring the contact's success. As contacts and messages become more tailored to specific customers, reflecting the individual customer's preferences and context, the probability for errors grows, as does the cost of recovery. The probability of errors also increases as products, services, delivery, payments, and fulfillment grow more flexible.

Orchestrating the best outcome from stage-to-stage and department-to-department is critical, not only to satisfy customer needs, but also to realize the optimum yield per customer, per contact, and per message slot.

Figure 5.4 Departments-Customer Contacts

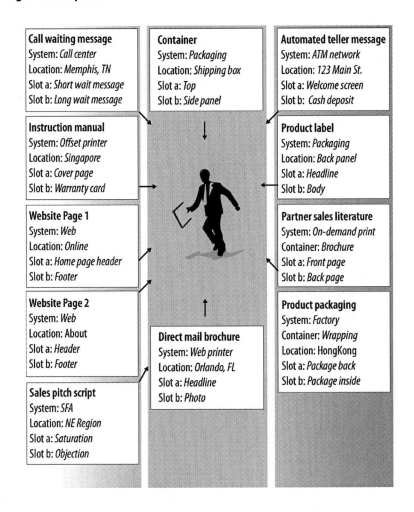

The Systems and Processes View

"Can't Find My Order"—Our Systems are Down View

The CxC Matrix Systems View (Figure 5.5) provides a summarized diagram depicting the resources and capabilities required to meet each customer's expectations. Even this summarized customer story lists 18 different systems managed by a mix of 17 departments and partners.

This level of System View explains the inter-company operations required to meet a customer's needs. The view should be easily understandable by everyone in the company without requiring them to have information technology, software, domain, or vendor knowledge.

The Systems View can be expanded to a much greater level of detail to expose each specific system and the system's functionality. System contact expansions can expose individual transactions, processes, fields, field values, business rules, and treatments. This level of information is not necessary across every system for every contact, but should be used when evaluating alternative system solutions, upgrading or replacing a system, outsourcing a system or function, or critiquing the company's capabilities and performance for a set of contacts.

Figure 5.5 Customer Process

CxC stage	Need		Shop		Buy		Use
	Awareness	Information	Selection	Negotiation	Contract	Logistics	Support
Customer view	receive email offer	search research	standard or deluxe	free for 90 days	terms & conditions	receive product	product query
Depart-ment	• marketing & ecommerce	• marketing web • PPC agency • product management • partners	• product management • ecommerce • operations • distribution	• product management • sales • finance	• sales • legal • finance	• operations • distribution • shipping • partner	• customer care • operations • training
System	• campaign management • database • email	• content management • website management • social networking	• ecommerce • ERP • inventory • management	• contract management • business process management • rules engine	• contract management • ecommerce • order management • inventory management	• vendor management • order management • email	• customer relationship management • intelligent router • resource management • VOIP

The graphic below (Figure 5.6) provides a conceptual view of one company's customer architecture and includes all of the systems responsible for delivering customer contacts. This high level customer architecture view is often used by department managers, information technology managers, and vendors to initiate discussions about inter-operability, system and data integration, system and function outsourcing and new technologies, and vendor software, service, and outsourcing possibilities.

Figure 5.6 Customer Architecture View

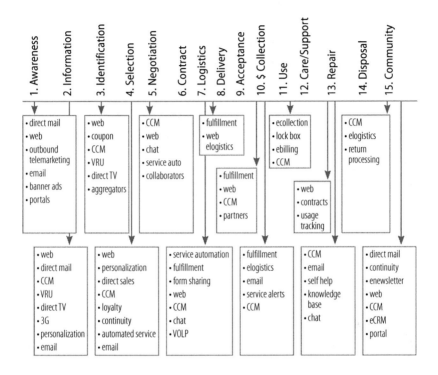

Infusing each contact with corporate objectives

This is where technology departments, operations, and business managers unite their resources, talents, and innovations to execute each contact and transaction with purpose and with specific and measurable revenue objectives.

The previous CxC Matrix levels depict the state of a company's customer experience "as is." But the CxC Matrix challenges businesses to manage and grow the value in each consumer stage by setting objectives, identifying the requirements for meeting specified objectives, and quantifying and measuring the value of each stage and contact.

Figure 5.7 Business Objectives

CxC stage	Need		Shop		Buy		Use
	Awareness	Information	Selection	Negotiation	Contract	Logistics	Support
Customer view	receive email offer	search research	standard or deluxe	free for 90 days	terms & conditions	receive product	product query
Depart-ment	• marketing & ecommerce	• marketing web • ppc agency • product management • partners	• product management • ecommerce • operations • distribution	• product management • sales • finance	• sales • legal • finance	• operations • distribution • shipping • partner	• customer care • operations • training
System	• campaign management • database email	• content management • website • management • social networking	• ecommerce • erp • inventory • management	• contract management • business process • management • rules engine	• contract management • ecommerce • order management • inventory management	• vendor management • order management • email	• customer relationship management • intelligent router • resource management • VOIP
Objective	a. promote store visit b. buy immediately	• up-sell • promote brand, service	• up-sell • promote store visit	• up-sell • cross-sell • service agreement	• extend warranty • loyalty enrollment	• efficiency • cross-sell • referral	• efficiency • cross-sell • referral • loyalty enrollment
Require-ment	• offer management • email list • content	• personalized • web • in-store visibility • localization • web cookie	• site search • email cookie • offer visibility	• customer profile • order/offer management system • credit score • customer id	• dynamic order management • process • training • enrollment • access	• resource visibility • training • incentive program • referral capture	• intelligent call routing • training • incentives • offer prompts
Value	• promotion • cost potential value	• search management cost • content cost • affiliate cost • affiliate/ partner gain share	• promotion cost • projected cross-sell revenue • affiliate revenue	• 15% increase close success • add-on revenue • fees	• revenue • entry costs • affiliate fees	• delivery cost • service fees • referral bonus	• cost per minute • offer cost • incentive cost • projected revenue

By exposing the systems, departments, and parties accountable for each contact, executives can clearly mandate objectives to the specific managers responsible for accomplishing them at each contact.

Business objectives may start out simply as "reduce cost" or "introduce service." These objectives may be dynamically modified by business, environment, and market circumstances.

Measuring performance contact-by-contact—
customer contact flow depicts company success

The Matrix delivers a quick view of customer flow and the success of each customer stage and contact channel. We do this in order to identify where we have specific contact opportunities to grow revenue and reduce cost.

In this way, the entire company can gather around and ask simple questions like, "How many customers in Stage One (Awareness) move to Stage Two (Information)?" Nothing is simpler.

Figure 5.8 Customer Conversion Rate

CUSTOMER LIFE STAGE

CHANNEL	Awareness	Selection	Purchase	Use	Support	Repair	Dispose
Dealer	X	X	X			X	X
Retail						X	X
Events	X	X					
Field sales							
Call center		X		X	X		
Web	X	X	X	X	X		
Email	X		X	X	X		
Direct mail	X						
Magazine	X						
Newspaper	X						
Radio							
TV	X						
Outdoor	X						
Community	X	X			X	X	X

| 30% | 25% | 70% | 90% | 20% | 15% |

The percentages show the survivor rate from stage to stage as described above—they are at the bottom to show the overall survivor rate versus the survivor rate in each cell.

The potential value of each contact is explicitly measured by the number of customers who pass through the contact and the downstream revenue, margin, and cost associated with each customer who experienced that contact.

Harness the power of your customer

Core to the CxC Matrix is monetizing each contact. Beyond simply tracking the sequence of contacts, the CxC Matrix calculates each contact's net financial impact. This is called "monetization."

Each contact is monetized by looking at its cost and breaking it into both cost and revenue components. Remember:

- Each contact bears a cost.
- Each contact has potential revenue, which is related to the customer's potential value.

The contact cost includes the cost of the channel/medium, the resources required for crafting and delivering the message, and all of the fixed and variable costs associated with contact handling.

You should assign costs to each contact in order to understand and quantify the impact of changes in customer flow, changes in transactional or per item costs, and alternative resource and processes options.

A CxC Matrix completed with costs-per-contact filled in clearly shows the cost advantage of Internet and self-service channels, as well as other lower-cost contact configurations. However, when customer flow is overlaid onto the cost Matrix, you can see when customers gravitate to lower-cost channels and when they prefer higher-cost options. The Matrix provides a realistic view that usually shows that first time customers initially conduct business through one combination of contacts, while repeat customers adopt another combination of contacts across the stages of their consumer cycle.

The CxC Cost Matrix provides a set of tools to depict hypothetical contact sequence scenarios using estimated customer flow and contact counts. It also provides a means for testing and observing service and contact configuration alternatives.

Figure 5.9 Estimated Costs for Contacts

Cost per purchased name	$ 0.10	–	$150.00
In-person sales call	$40.00	–	$500.00
Group presentation	$350.00	–	$3,000.00
Self-service interaction	$0.01	–	$0.40
At-home sales call	$25.00	–	$150.00
Outbound telemarketing	$8.00	–	$35.00
Fax/mail	$3.00	–	$5.00
Inside sales call	$20.00	–	$100.00
Inbound telephone support	$4.00	–	$75.00
Direct mail	$0.25	–	$12.00
Email	$0.03	–	$0.60
Inbound referral	$20.00	–	$500.00
Trade show	$100.00	–	$6,000.00
Internal website	$0.15	–	$12.00
Third-party web	$0.05	–	$200.00
Partner sale	$1.00	–	$100,000.00

The Matrix provides a means to quantify each contact's contribution to a customer's propensity to purchase, as well as projections for probable expense and contacts post-sale.

The CxC Matrix requires that every customer contact be inventoried, monetized, analyzed, and prioritized.

The Simplest Measure

One of the reasons that the CxC Matrix is so powerful is that it stems from one key measure: did the customer buy something? In the case of the

Matrix, this means that success is measured by getting customers to CxC Matrix Stage Six: Contract. Every other contact has an explicit cost and only potential revenue.

Stage Six, **Contract,** is the pivotal moment by which we can measure the success of all prior stages. For this reason, we measure the success of each stage from one through five by the percentage of customers who pass from stage to stage.

The Company View—monetization and "the mower"

Examining the mower program from the company's perspective uncovers an enormous number of contacts and the successful and unsuccessful contact attempts made by the company and the targeted customers.

Employees who are not in marketing or sales can better understand their customer's mindset when they become aware of all of the messages the company directs at customers to generate sales.

The mower campaign targeted 20,000 customers, of which 180 or 0.9 percent actually bought a targeted item (mower, hedge clippers, or barbecue grill). An additional 230 targeted customers bought something during the promotion period, but their purchases were not directly attributable to this campaign.

For the 180 customers who made the target purchase, there were 4,000 customers who did not receive the email; 6,300 received the email but did not open it. Another 8,900 customers opened the email but did not click on the highlighted section that would have taken them to the company website. Eight hundred customers clicked the link, and 270 of them spent more than three minutes on the site viewing individual product pages. Thirty of the website visitors bought the targeted product directly from the website. Four customers went through the entire purchasing process on the website up to the point in the checkout process when the system requested their credit card number. Then they abandoned the purchase. Thirty-two customers went directly to Google from the web page and searched for the featured item.

Figure 5.10 Surviving Customers/Leftover Potential

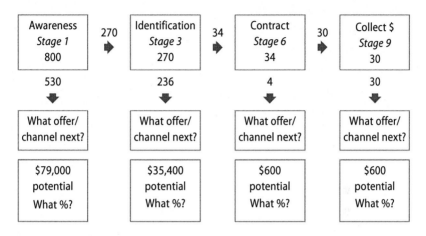

Potential assumes $150 per customer; "What %?" calculates next offer success rate.

The Matrix provides a means to quantify each contact's contribution to a customer's propensity to purchase, as well as projections for probable expense and contacts post-sale.

The rear view window — How did we get here?

The Matrix also correlates service, delivery, repair, and support costs and activities with earlier customer contacts. So, in addition to calculating the cost of each incident and the cumulative cost of customer acquisition— Matrix stages one through six—the Matrix provides insight into which channels and contacts drive up post-sales expenses. The more detailed Matrix views and models provide all of the components of the customer experience, delivering even more information about potential causes and effects of each prior customer contact.

Figure 5.11 Customer Flow, SCP

	Geography	Digital	Location	Third party	One-on-one	Community	Total customers per stage	Customer flow	SCP $
1. Awareness	1,400	400	300	150	800	3,050	6,100		
2. Information	1,000	145	250	62	650	2,117	933	30.59%	$156,600
3. Identification	900	95	180	49	420	1644	473	22.34%	$48,600
4. Selection	600	70	35	44	350	1,099	545	33.15%	$95,000
5. Negotiation	250	62	10	40	60	422	677	61.60%	$77,400
6. Contract	145	58	4	28	0	235	187	44.31%	$25,400
7. Logistics	145	50	4	28	11	238	-3	-1.28%	$1,600
8. Delivery	138	47	2	20	21	228	10	4.20%	$4,000
9. Acceptance	130	47	2	19	21	219	9	3.95%	$1,800
10. $ Collection	145	50	4	28	27	254	-35	-15.98%	-$5,800
11. Use	130	45	4	19	390	588	-334	-131.50%	$5,800
12. Care/Support	40	12	0	7	580	638	-51	-8.67%	$27,800
13. Repair	21	4	0	2	210	237	402	62.91%	$6,400
14. Dispose	9	4	1	1	41	56	181	76.37%	$2,400
15. Community	130	80	28	41	3,400	3,679			

In the more detailed case on the prior page (Figure 5.10), the company estimates that each customer is worth $200 in profits. This number is used to quickly observe the opportunity available from stage to stage: SCP (Stage Channel Potential) = the potential additional revenue available per CxC Matrix stage. SCP factors customer value times the customer's propensity to buy based on similar customers performance.

Note: *Total Customers* counts the identifiable customers excluding anonymous shoppers/visitors and de-duplicating customers appearing in multiple channels within the same customer stage.

These numbers represent a subset of customers that entered the CxC Matrix on the same day then follows the group for 126 days, the company's calculated customer lifetime. All values are based on individual company benchmarks.

The opportunity can be further drilled down to channel, medium, system, offer, and so forth.

This simple, customer-count-populated Matrix (Figure 5.11) shows the rate at which customers move from stage to stage, and it represents the company's success in closing sales from the customers in stages one through five. It also shows the customers who fail to move to a subsequent stage, while also quantifying the total forfeited value lost at each stage.

While no company converts 100 percent of its customers from stage to stage, this Matrix view quickly monetizes the potential value resident in each cell—stage and channel combination—and provides an estimate of the total amount of profit to be gained by creating incremental improvements at each customer stage and contact. The detailed contact view shows the potential profit resident in each cell, which managers can use to make investment decisions regarding the tactics best suited to grow performance. The same Matrix view then provides ongoing monitoring of tactical success.

Monetization is a primary benefit of the CxC Matrix because it links specific business decisions, that is, which messages to present and what their content should be, to long-term customer value.

The monetization of contacts—the core concept of the CxC Matrix—is implemented through the monetization of slots.

Companies generally assess the cost of an employee's completion of a task such as the per-item cost of billing, ordering, inventory, delivery, shelf space, and so forth. Some companies go so far as to calculate expenses associated with assessing customer fitness or worthiness through customer verifications, credit checks, demographics and segmentations, and customer file assessments, but few try to assess a customer's "future value" by estimating the amount of revenue the customer will generate over a lifetime.

The Matrix highlights where your customer ceases to have contacts, providing a date stamp and all of the earlier contact activities. The stages where most customers are lost should be examined for corrective action and treatments that grow revenue. Using customer lifetime value as a metric, you can calculate the benefits of improving individual Matrix cell performance by estimating the increase in customers who move through to the contract stage.

Recommended CxC Matrix monetization applications

Strategy

Value calculations can help make major investment decisions such as whether to expand plant capacity, launch a new product line, or change service levels. Managers construct a scenario for each option and compare the expected values. Unlike scenarios built using conventional techniques, scenarios based on the CxC Matrix ensure that all implications of a given choice are considered. For example, a model for adding a new product line would include the expected change in customer service volume. This helps to avoid unanticipated results that can reduce or even reverse the benefits of a superficially attractive option.

Revenue Enhancement

Every customer contact is an opportunity to increase customer value. By assigning an explicit value to the contact, monetization encourages more efficient use of contacts that may be executed with little thought or ignored altogether. For example, many firms never think to include advertisements in packages they ship to customers. Others throw in a copy of their catalog but don't measure the resulting sales. Only a handful of companies are thorough enough to measure the value of sales from their own catalog and compare it with revenue they would generate if a third party paid to insert its materials instead. A comprehensive inventory of customer contacts uncovers more opportunities than most businesses realize, from Google ad placement on a website, to messages embedded in call-on-hold scripts, to cross-sell offers made at the close of a customer service inquiry to simply asking your customers whether they know the name of someone else that could benefit from your products and services.

Operations

Because monetization calculates the change in long-term value resulting from each contact, it gives operational managers a way to measure their group's contribution to the entire organization. This avoids the departmental myopia that can lead to decisions that are good for one area but harmful to the larger organization. For example, a purchasing organization might find it can save money by using a lower quality supplier, even after allowing for direct impacts such as increased service costs, higher returns, and larger warranty expenses. But a comprehensive customer value analysis would include impacts on other departments, such as lower revenues from loss of repeat business, fewer sales of other company products, and fewer referrals by enthusiastic customers. This might result in a different decision that is ultimately better for the company as a whole.

Forecasting

Exposing the impact of each customer contact creates a company-wide network of risks and opportunity sensors that enable execution nimbleness.

The financial measures underlying monetization are based on projections of non-financial measures such as advertising impressions, sales calls, contact center call volumes, website visits, opened emails, metered product and service usage, and purchase quantities. These can be used to build budgets and forecasts. Because the budgets are based on projections for specific inputs, financial variances can also be traced to specific sources.

Improved Predictive Model Performance

Traditional forecasts are often based on statistical models that predict results without describing the underlying business activities that cause them. This makes it much harder to analyze the causes of any deviations. Similarly, because the CxC Matrix projects customer activities over time, any revised projections automatically include the future impact of past variances. Thus, a shortfall in sales this quarter will automatically result in lower projections for service calls in the future, making it easier for companies to understand the true implications of their current results.

CHAPTER 6

Managing Customers Contact-by-Contact

Up to this point, we have charted one customer's footsteps through the Matrix to illustrate how the Matrix's core elements operate. But the Matrix is designed to provide insight into how each element in every customer contact performs across your company's entire customer base.

The contact and experience permutations portrayed in the CxC Matrix are staggering when you consider the potential number of combinations of messages, slots, containers, variable attributes, and customers across each customer life stage. This is the challenge the Matrix is designed to meet. It provides insight and management capability for each message in each slot in each contact.

Mindset and a toolset

The CxC Matrix is the foundation of the Think Like a Customer (TLC) management methodology that encourages all employees and stakeholders to be customer-centric, designing every business decision around the customer, while emphasizing strict measurement and company-wide transparency. The methodology strives to connect business strategy and objectives to customer contacts and activities.

The process is designed to provide everyone in your company with a view of their role as it relates to customers, while providing a means to document decision-making guidelines, procedures, and standards to govern each customer contact. The TLC method provides a means for companies to realize the optimum return per customer contact and is designed to work in conjunction with existing performance measures, systems, and policies.

Visualize the customer experience

Before you can affect customer performance, your company must collectively understand its customers' experiences.

One of the visual Matrix's greatest benefits is that it invites participation and innovation from the broadest spectrum of employees at a company.

Figure 6.1 Customer Process

CUSTOMER PROCESS						
Awareness	Selection	Purchase	Use	Support	Repair	Dispose
X	X	X			X	X
					X	X
X	X					
	X		X	X		
X	X	X	X	X		
X		X	X	X		
X						
X						
X						
X						
X						
X	X			X	X	X

BUSINESS PROCESS

The outcome of each contact, where the business process intersects the customer process, is determined by the decisions used to conduct each contact. Result is, ultimately, lifetime value: (direct revenue + affiliate revenue + referrals) − cumulative contacts cost.

"Our life is frittered away by detail. Simplify, simplify!" —Henry David Thoreau

---

When designing or rethinking the design of any system, it helps if everyone involved has a "picture" of what is being proposed. Unlike an engineering drawing, the CxC Matrix is designed to:

1. Provide a visual picture of the intersection of customer stages and company processes.

2. Help identify potential customer interaction system shortfalls.

CxC Matrix components and mechanics

Fifteen Customer Stages Mirror the Customer Journey

The 15 Matrix stages in the consumer cycle are designed to align with standard corporate functions including technology systems, process designs, department responsibilities, in-house and outsourced service arrangements, and standard metrics, such as Six Sigma, APQC, or National Retail Federation. Although the standard set of CxC Matrix stages cover a wide range of businesses, other labels could be used if they were more appropriate to a particular situation.

The Matrix stages generally occur in a fixed sequence from left to right on the standard Matrix diagram. But there will always be exceptions. A damaged product may be replaced before it is used or a product purchased on credit may be delivered before payment is collected. A customer may repeat portions of the sequence, for example, by selecting an alternate product if negotiations on the initial selection are unsuccessful. There may be multiple contacts within the same stage—most buyers make several visits to a house before they buy it.

In more complex purchases and particularly business purchases, where the buyer may be a multi-party entity, individual stages may be managed by separate departments or multiple departments and people. For example, a company may decide that it requires a larger office space, so it establishes a committee to evaluate options, gather information regarding alternatives, review and narrow choices, and negotiate the purchase or lease.

In this case, a seller or broker may be dealing with a subset of the decision-making entity and likely cannot see the breadth of the customer's available choices nor the full breadth of the customer's collective needs.

Figure 6.2

1. Awareness	2. Information	3. Identification	4. Selection	5. Negotiation	6. Contract	7. Logistics	8. Delivery	9. Acceptance	10. $ Collection	11. Use	12. Care/Support	13. Repair	14. Disposal	15. Community

1. *Customer becomes aware of need*

2. *Customer gathers information regarding filling the need*

3. *Customer identifies potential options and sources to satisfy need*

4. *Customer selects product(s), service(s), provider(s), to satisfy need requirements*

5. *Customer negotiates all aspects of acquiring product or service*

6. *Customer legally commits to product purchase and specifications*

7. *Customer establishes criteria for receipt*

8. *Product or service is delivered to customer*

9. *Customer accepts or rejects product/service*

10. *Customer pays for product and/or services*

11. *Customer uses product*

12. *Customer cares for product, learns about product*

13. *Customer fixes, repairs product*

14. *Customer disposes, sells, destroys product*

15. *Customer participates in "word-of-mouth" product/service community*

Stage 1: Awareness is the customer's starting point. The customer has made the decision to make an investment of his or her time and interest in pursuing something. The customer has a need, although perhaps not a clearly defined need. It may be generated by a feeling, a curiosity, a life event, a situation, a desire to replace something, a whim, an urge, or an impulse.

Email spam does not count as a "contact" . . . unless a customer reads it

Your company pays to generate billions of customer contacts through advertising, public relations, email blasts, telemarketing, and unattended events such as webinars, webcasts, online videos, or fax on demand. The customer's awareness and participation in the activity is essential. If the customer does not see the email because it is blocked, the contact is not counted by either the customer or the CxC Matrix. If a telemarketer does not speak to a customer or leaves a message that the customer deletes immediately, the contact is not counted. If an advertising insert in an envelope is discarded without ever being viewed, it is not counted.

In order for a customer to be counted in the awareness stage, the customer must have some activity, known or anonymous, in that stage. The customer must participate.

Inference

Some customers are not individually identifiable until "Stage 3: Identification" or at "Stage 5: Negotiation," choosing to remain anonymous while conducting earlier stages. For example, the customer may have worked with a third party or broker, or he may have worked anonymously, through the web, a pseudonym, or another less detectable means.

A customer who suddenly appears in a stage without links to prior stages, especially a first-time customer, may also indicate fraud. For example, a customer may appear in the repair stage, requesting a refund, or appear at Stage 12: Care and Support, with no record of a purchase.

CxC Matrix channels

Channels represent the physical, digital, and virtual locations where customer contacts occur. A sample list includes call centers, retail stores, email messages, invoices, web review sites, delivery labels, packaging, websites, magazine ads, coupons, chat rooms, in-field sales agents, welcome screen messages, partners, promotional items, independent resellers, the product and service itself, wholesalers, outsourced customer contact centers, the ever-expanding array of electronic customer-to-company contact points, and every vehicle in which a customer has contact with a product or brand and the product or brand's image, mention, and effects.

Figure 6.3 Mapping the Customer Journey by Channel

		1. Awareness	2. Information	3. Identification	4. Selection	5. Negotiation	6. Contract	7. Logistics	8. Delivery	9. Acceptance	10. $ Collection	11. Use	12. Care & Support	13. Repair	14. Dispose	15. Community
Geography	TV															
	Community events															
	Radio															
	Outdoor															
	Signage															
	Magazines															
Digital	Banner ads															
	Website															
	Company email															
	Campaign management email															
	Support email															
	Sales click for chat															
Location	In-store promotions															
	Kiosks															
Third party	Package inserts															
	Private-label partners															
	Affiliate offers															
One-on-one	Inbound telemartketing															
	Online customer support															
	Billing statements															
	Shipments															
	Door-to-door															
	Catalog															
	Customer service															
	Statement inserts															
	Service click for chat															
	Direct mail															
	Outbound telemartketing															
Community	Press/trade magazines															
	Blogs															
	Craigslist.com															

The high level CxC Matrix classifies channels into six categories that closely represent customers' expectations for **service, intimacy,** and **urgency**: Geography, Digital, Location, Third Party, One-on-One, and Community.

CxC Matrix channel categories—fast-easy-simple

Figure 6.4 CxC Matrix

	1. Awareness	2. Information	3. Identification	4. Selection	5. Negotiation	6. Contract	7. Logistics	8. Delivery	9. Acceptance	10. $ Collection	11. Use	12. Care/Support	13. Repair	14. Disposal	15. Community
Geography															
Digital															
Location															
Third party															
One-on-one															
Community															

Where do I go from here?

These broad channel categories represent starting points for the customer as well as for constructing a CxC Matrix. Imagine, again, thinking like a customer. How do I begin to search for your product or service? I likely search online (digital), go to a store, office, or mall (location), call a friend, peer, or advisor (community), contact a current vendor or reseller (third party), or open a catalog, email, or contact from my past (one-on-one). Customers have different expectations for service, convenience, time, and intimacy based on which channel category they choose to contact the company. A customer has different expectations when asking questions face to face in a store or at an office in Stage 3: Identification, versus when shopping online. The customer has different expectations for what can be accomplished, the timeliness and thoroughness of a product presentation, and the question and answer exchange.

Figure 6.5 Types of Advertising Trusted by Internet Users Worldwide, April 2007 (% of respondents)

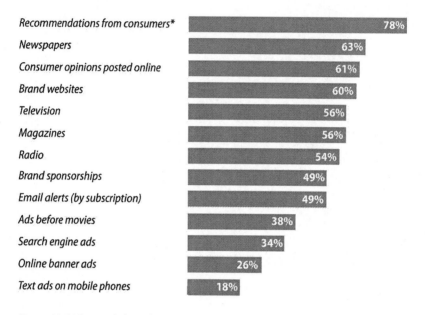

Recommendations from consumers*	78%
Newspapers	63%
Consumer opinions posted online	61%
Brand websites	60%
Television	56%
Magazines	56%
Radio	54%
Brand sponsorships	49%
Email alerts (by subscription)	49%
Ads before movies	38%
Search engine ads	34%
Online banner ads	26%
Text ads on mobile phones	18%

Note: n=26,486; *i.e., word-of-mouth

Source: The Nielsen Company, "Online Global Consumer Study" as cited in press release, October 1, 2007, www.eMarketer.com

It is the customer view—you live where?

A customer's experience is consistently influenced by his environment, and I define this environment a couple of different ways:

Geography

Weather, seasons, laws, politics, convenience, distance to location—all of these related issues affect a customer's experience from the requirement to use a product to the product's attributes. Do I need air conditioning in my car? Is a convertible practical? What about snow tires?

Contact vehicles in the geography channel category include newspapers, broadcast and regional television, sales and distribution territories, and fulfillment and delivery networks such as postal routes, delivery routes, sales territories, distribution licenses, service agreements, travel routes, and licensing conditions.

Digital

Includes the set of contacts a customer has via the World Wide Web or web-connected device such as a wireless phone, personal digital assistant (PDA), in-vehicle navigation and information systems, and blast email or other unaddressed electronic message vehicles.

For example, a customer can access a company website and spend time navigating and searching, or downloading information without logging in or providing any personal information. This anonymous activity is classified in the digital category. Once the customer enters personal information, which may or may not identify that customer as a current customer or return visitor, the category shifts to one-on-one. While companies may use web session cookies and other means to track returning customers and capture web and other digital exposures, the contacts are classified as digital until the customer acknowledges identification or a desire to be identified.

The digital channel category does not typically include addressable electronic contacts, opt-in electronic messages, email, text messages, or messages delivered via registered website visits, which are classified in the one-on-one channel category.

Location

Includes the set of contacts that take place in a store, office, trade show booth, kiosk, or other single, fixed, physical location. It is best to think of channels in the location category as destinations: physical places the customer must travel to. In some cases, customers and company representatives must each travel to a location to meet, such as a trade show.

Third Party

Includes all addressable third party entities that sell, resell, distribute, influence, and review a company's products and services. Addressable means that the company has direct communication and a formal or informal relationship/dialogue with the third party. For example, resellers, non-captive sales agents, registered financing companies, all forms of registered partners and vendors, news editors/advertorials, paid reviewers, and analysts are classified in the third party category.

One-on-One

Includes all direct contacts with a customer that appear to be personalized and bi-directional from the customer's perspective. One-om-One contacts require individual customer information and often make use of some customer database, contact management system, or integrated access of multiple sales, operations, order management, contact management, and other systems.

Community

Includes all of the channels and contacts that exist outside a company's control: word-of-mouth mentions, product and service reviews, news, and press exposures, social networking, web forums, unplanned product and service exposure, after-market sales and contacts, inter-customer bartering, trading, collecting, fan and hater clubs, websites, independent and unsponsored user groups, independent sellers, re-packagers, aggregators, disaggregators and their sales, service, refurbishing, refinishing, and repair networks.

Customers exist in communities where they exchange information with people of similar interests and needs. A person with a need often seeks a community solution through a referral, recommendation, or other word-of-mouth means for assessing purchase, usage, and care options.

"A person like me" has become the most credible source of information about a company or a product, increasing from **20% in 2003 to 68% today."**

—Edelman Trust Barometer

Community: Life Stage 15 and Channel Domain

- 39% of the online population, 57 million American adults, regularly read blogs
- Approximately 175,000 new blogs are created each day
- Approximately 1.6 million blog posts are made per day, equivalent to 18 posts per second

Source: Pew Internet; Technorati

The importance of community

Community has always been a major source of customer contacts. Community is the place where customers exchange their experiences about product and service performance, quality, price, product use, customer service, and adventures.

Communities used to be considered primarily as organic, local groups for customers with similar interests who were bound by proximity and communication restraints. With advances in the World Wide Web and communication channels, special interest groups, and hobbyists, all sorts of people can inexpensively (and without restraint) attack brands, companies, products, and industries. Advances in web technologies enable customers to not only exchange stories and commentary, but also purchase, service, resell, and execute contacts across every Matrix stage via the community channel. Customers can buy on Amazon, Craigslist, or eBay and receive customer support from a self-described fan or fan group in a web forum or blog. They can receive expert product use and repair advice and services through websites like Elance, ITToolbox, Angieslist, Guru.com, Getafreelance, or TDWI. Customers have access to thousands of community category channels.

Think Like a Customer!
Matrix contacts retail banking breadcrumb trail

Even a simple Matrix like the banking one below, representing a banking customer's contact activity for the past 30 days, clearly shows which channels the customer prefers to use for different activities. Just as importantly, it shows which channels he or she prefers not to use. Gaining better understanding of how customers use contacts to conduct their business with your company illuminates opportunities for designing new services and service combinations and configurations, while also excluding or reducing investment in other contact areas.

Figure 6.6

CHANNEL	Awareness	Selection	Purchase	Use	Support	Repair	Dispose
Branch	X	X	X			X	X
Retail						X	X
Events	X	X					
Field sales							
Call center		X		X	X		
Web	X	X	X	X	X		
Email	X		X	X	X		
Direct mail	X						
Magazine	X						
Newspaper	X						
Radio							
TV	X						
Outdoor	X						
Community	X	X			X	X	X

This customer received messages trying to up-sell and cross-sell services through eleven awareness generating channels. He then used a combination of the branch, the online bank, an event and the call center to research and select a service. He also performed some research about the bank's community involvement prior to attempting to purchase a service at the branch, through the online banking service, and by email. The customer had some problem with the account as evidenced by the combination of support and repair contacts before he closed his account and cancelled his new service in the branch after trying to close his account at the ATM. He started complaining about the bank's service on Facebook while contacting support, where he also discussed his repair and disposal sentiments.

What about eBay and *The New York Times?*

How certain third-party channels are classified may depend upon how your company uses them more than how the customer perceives the channel's operation. For example, a customer in search of a particular machine part may search on Google and find a seller at eBay, along with search links from the part manufacturer, a number of reseller distributors, and miscellaneous after-market providers. The customer may choose the eBay seller based on price and shipping terms without knowing that the seller is actually the manufacturer. This manufacturer simply chose to leverage eBay as a sales channel, but it is not obligated under the same warranty or service requirements as it is when it sells the product part directly. So, what appears as a set of community contacts to the customer may actually be third-party contacts through eBay.

In a similar instance, a favorable product mention and review in an article may appear to a customer as unbiased, unscripted advice. Therefore, it appears to be a community contact. But if the review is written from information provided in a press release where the company may or may not also be an advertiser in the publication, sometimes referred to as an "advertorial," the customer's reading of the review should be classified as a third-party contact.

"If you make customers unhappy in the physical world, they might each tell 6 friends. If you make customers unhappy on the Internet, they can each tell 6,000 friends."

—Jeff Bezos, Amazon

Experience Matrix communities—clarity through chaos

In the past, individuals in communities had faint voices and small impact through word-of-mouth, only gaining recognition when they got louder through a published letter to the editor or commentary in some other broadcast media. Today, individuals regularly create tremendous influence through user-generated media like blogs, YouTube, Facebook, Twitter, user forums, chat commentary, and a growing number of social networking venues.

While your company's investment and participation in community may have been seen as insignificant or arbitrary in the past, Internet and digital communications have changed company and community relations forever.

Your managers might ask, "Why pay attention to community?" Since communities by definition are unmanaged, uncontrollable, and unpredictable, why bother? Because communities can be influenced, persuaded and leveraged. Communities can be put to work not just to get the word out, but also to create "the word" and package and deliver a message.

"Up to 25% of the entertainment being consumed in five years will be what we call 'circular'. . . people will have a genuine desire not only to create and share their own content, but also to remix it, mash it up, and pass it on within their peer groups."

—Mark Selby, Vice President Multimedia, Nokia, December 2007

Angry and exuberant customer messages can make or break a new market entry, a product, or a brand. This challenges you to continually maintain awareness of what is being said about your company in multiple channels and to remain alert to changes in community sentiments. Resources and messages must be prepared at every contact point to ensure that the right message and response is delivered.

The CxC Matrix helps you measure the impact of communities on all of the other channels and customer stages.

As a channel, communities cross-pollinate information with other channels such as digital, geography, and third party. Message and information artifacts are spread through word-of-mouth and customer folklore. Customers tell stories of alternate uses for products or how they received exceptional service under the direst circumstances.

The CxC Matrix treats "community" as both a stage in the consumer cycle and a channel since customers freely contribute information and commentary to communities while they access information from communities throughout their customer experiences.

Companies traditionally participate in communities through third parties and in external activities, as well as under the budget categories of "public relations" and "charitable giving." While these types of community givebacks may be truly altruistic, your company measurably benefits from the local visibility that sways public sentiment, particularly in times of corporate trouble or when seeking approval from local politicians and special interest groups. A common justification for spending in the community is helping to promote a positive brand image.

Customers know when companies are lying

Walmart's public relations firm thought it had a good idea. Why not create a blog in which an average American couple travels across America in a recreational vehicle and stays in Walmart parking lots? Many middle-class Americans would relate to their adventures and get a warm, fuzzy feeling about Walmart as a place to shop. The problem was that nowhere on the blog was it revealed that Walmart was paying for all the expenses of the blogging couple. It didn't take long for the promotional tactic to be revealed and brought to a halt.

In faking a blog, Walmart and its advertising agency was experimenting in a new channel category—community—where rules of engagement and disclosure have not yet been clearly defined. They certainly exposed the need to distinguish paid advertising and paid storytelling from user-contributed blogs and stories.

Similar mistakes frequently happen in the digital community. Product and company reviews sometimes seem a little too clean, polished, and detailed to believe that an average customer took the time and effort to write them on a whim. Certainly, some customers do write extensive, fact-laden reviews and commentary, but if fewer than three percent of customers ever report complaints, imagine the odds of a customer writing a review, let alone a comprehensive product walk-through.

It's one thing for a company to write a review. It's a whole other thing for a company to delete community information.

"On November 17th, 2005, an anonymous Wikipedia user deleted 15 paragraphs from an article on e-voting machine-vendor Diebold, excising an entire section critical of the company's machines. While anonymous, such changes typically leave behind digital fingerprints offering hints about the contributor, such as the location of the computer used to make the edits. In this case, the changes came from an IP address reserved for the corporate offices of Diebold itself. And it is far from an isolated case. A new data-mining service ... traces millions of Wikipedia entries to their corporate sources, and, for the first time, puts comprehensive data behind longstanding suspicions of manipulation, which until now have surfaced only piecemeal in investigations of specific allegations."

Source: John Borland, *Wired News*, August 19, 2007, © John Borland.

Company trust will continue to be tested as advocates, loyal customers, loyal employees, interested third parties, and competitors alike participate in anonymous communities to add and subtract stories and comments.

How powerful are digital communities?
I think they elected the President of the United States

The power of leveraging communities to achieve a specific goal was evident in the 2008 United States Presidential Election. Barack Obama enlisted a digital community of over five million "friends" across a network of social networking sites and his own hosted site, MyBarackObama. The Obama campaign leveraged the "unmanageable" channels by providing a variety of tools and gadgets in each of the digital spaces to help individuals take ownership of the campaign's popular messages.

The campaign provided content to be shared and modified using each web platform's technologies, including notes, photos, news feeds, posted items, video messages, tags, event posts, invitations, friend requests, profile pages, and fan walls. It fueled a motivated audience and leveraged all of the viral aspects of the digital community while likely educating a lot of new users to the many "cool" technical capabilities in each application.

The immediate statistics are overwhelming:

Community	McCain	Obama
Facebook	620,359	2,379,102
MySpace: Friends	217,811	833,161
Twitter: Followers	4,603	112,474
YouTube: Channel Views	2,032,993	18,413,110

Additionally, MyBarackObama hosted over two million profiles, connected 200,000 offline events, and served nearly half a million blog posts.

Channel and media expectations differ from customer to company

HURRY I REALLY NEED HELP WITH MY CHECKING ACCOUNT: texting is fastest right? No? How about email? No? Then what . . .

On its website, PNC Bank tells customers not to submit text messages or emails to the bank because they may be intercepted by third parties or not received by appropriate business units at the bank. The bank asks customers to call its toll-free number or write instead.

This is not meant to ridicule PNC Bank. Most companies currently choose not to handle email, text messages, or other quick and easy channels with the urgency in which they are sent.

PNC discourages customers from using email as an contact channel to communicate with the bank, stating that it "may not be secure, may be intercepted." While these types of disclosures exist in small print in most contacts, it is unlikely that customers ever read them. This only causes greater customer frustration when the customer experiences the effects of "may not be immediately received by the appropriate business unit at PNC." The bank does not insert any caveats or warnings about sending a letter, nor does it ensure that the appropriate business unit will receive a letter. Just imagine the cost of manually handling each of these contacts and their follow-up. There must be a better way!

Of course, there are good reasons for discouraging certain contacts and practices, and the biggest reasons are cost and liability. The cost of customer service personnel to respond to text messages and emails is exorbitant, not to mention the cost and liability associated with emails that may have been blocked, email blasts designed to overwhelm companies, and so on. The list of excuses goes on and on.

Customers have different service, response, access, and intimacy expectations related to each CxC Matrix channel category and their needs at each stage in the consumer cycle. For example, a customer dealing one-on-one with a company by phone, chat, or even postal mail has different expectations of response time than a person who is face-to-face with a sales representative at a physical location. Likewise, if a customer is dealing with an online, third party intermediary looking to negotiate price on a large ticket item, the customer will have different expectations than if he is online on the company-managed order page or on the phone with the company's in-house service representative. Customers have different expectations in each channel for information (Can I try it on? Can I take it for a test drive?), identification (I have five websites open at the same time sorting each by price), product delivery, and payment terms.

Companies control some channels, whereas third parties own others. Channels may also be reached through other channels. For example, a website may be available through an in-store kiosk, and a call center may be reached at an airport check-in counter.

Contacts

Although the customer must be aware of your company's involvement in a contact, your company is not always aware of your customer. Contacts such as exposure to a public billboard, viewing an in-store product display, and daily product use can occur without your customer being identified. Even direct contacts, such as telephone inquiries, may not be recorded, or they may be recorded without linking them to a specific customer.

A benefit of the Matrix is that the need to identify contacts leads companies to consider new ways to record exposures and capture responses. This is a particularly important opportunity today when technologies such as Radio Frequency Identification (RFID) tags, self-diagnosis and repair functionality, and web-connected smart devices generate enormous amounts of data that can potentially be linked to customers.

"Wow me" — Every contact should be an "event"

"When the customer opens the box each month, we want it to be an event filled with excitement, curiosity, and pleasure. Each opening of the box must stick out in customers' memories. The coffee memory and the box memories are intertwined and critical to customer tenure and up-sells."

—Executive at major coffee membership company

Customers want to be wowed. They want to be impressed, acknowledged, entertained, and served in ways that merit attention, such as "opening the box." The box referred to above is from a company that delivers coffee on a periodic basis as part of a membership or continuity program. Coffee arrives at the customer's home or office based on the frequency specified by the customer. The box's exterior is brown and unexceptional except for a large color imprint of the brand's name. The company carefully selects and arranges the items in the box and plans the messages and sensory experiences that opening the box will generate.

The coffee company deliberately and effectively uses the box opening as a platform to reinvigorate the customer's perception of its brand. This measurably benefits customer retention, cross-sales, gift sales, and referrals. The company also includes additional offers in each box, using the customer's information, demographics, coffee consumption and taste preferences to determine which products and messages should be packed and in what order. For example, the box may contain a sweepstakes entry form if the customer's modeled profile indicates he responds to that sort of thing. The box may contain a sample of a new coffee or tea that is coming to market which might grow his monthly consumption. Each element of each box is carefully crafted to create the optimum customer response. It's designed to create a delighted, enthusiastic customer and ideally to prompt the customer to share the event with others by word-of-mouth, as a gift, or as a referral.

Some contacts should be memorable, but sometimes business models perform best when contacts go unnoticed. E-ZPass is one such example, where a customer's payment account is automatically debited each time the customer's vehicle passes through a highway toll booth or exits a parking lot that is a member of the E-ZPass payment network. E-ZPass makes the "collection" stage a non-event for its subscribers.

Summary

Contacts represent any connection between a customer and a company. The CxC Matrix classifies contacts along two major dimensions: channel and stages in the consumer cycle. Stage reflects customer needs and attributes, while channel represents company resources and behavior. Within a channel, contacts are further classified by container, system, and slot.

In the context of a given contact, each slot can be assigned a specific value representing its potential impact on the long-term value of the individual customer. Companies can optimize customer value by optimizing use of their slots. Treatments apply business rules to manage a contact's components and coordinate messages during each contact. Treatments are the mechanism to manage the customer experience and optimize relationship value.

CHAPTER 7

Nine Treatment Objectives for Each Contact

Every customer contact should strive to achieve the following nine objectives:

1. **Identify Customer:** "Repeat Customer," "First Time Customer," or "Anonymous"

2. **Recognize Customer:** connect customer's history, preferences, values

3. **Fulfill:** meet customer's original purpose for this contact

4. **Upgrade:** motivate customer to upgrade current product or service

5. **Cross-sell:** another product, service, or partner's service

6. **Expand:** invite customer to graduate to higher customer tier, i.e., loyalty program, newsletter/email sign-up, event invite, complete "my profile"

7. **Educate:** teach customer about the company, available channels, special interests, best practices, or how to use its products

8. **Collect:** data about the customer and experience

9. **Generate Referrals:** leverage the customer relationship to gather names of prospects

You should evaluate how well each contact meets a standard set of treatment objectives. This can identify opportunities for improvement and find misalignments between customer needs and actual treatments, as well as identify the contacts with the greatest potential for improvement.

You (should have) had me at "Hello"

Identify Customer

The first objective of each contact should be to establish whether the customer is a repeat customer, first time customer, anonymous, or other. Think of this as having caller ID at every customer contact point. This initial identification dictates the contact's messaging and objectives to best suit the customer's situation. If the customer is a repeat, then the system and container, person, website, and customer service representative (CSR) should readily be able to leverage the customer's history, stated preferences, and modeled preferences.

First time customers entering an experience stage have different expectations, needs, concerns, and questions than repeat customers. Anonymous and unidentifiable customers contacting sales or service or just shopping can only be assisted to the extent that they express their intentions and needs. They should be encouraged and motivated to register and identify themselves based on the benefits they will receive in future contacts.

Customer identification can occur in several forms from an automated screen pop-up on a website that says, "Welcome back! Would you like to continue from where you left off on your last visit?" or a confirmation screen or in-person introduction that asks, "First time customer?"

Recognize Customer

Once a customer has been identified, you should be able to access and use the customer's prior contacts, purchase history, and service history to inform the current contact of what should take place. At a minimum, it is important to know and acknowledge whether the customer had prior contacts and to somehow acknowledge the customer's investment of time and effort. Recognizing a customer may be as simple as a "Welcome back" greeting in a store followed by, "Are you still looking for the right blender?" It could involve making a reference to a previous purchase or service inquiry on the phone or on the web, followed by a relevant offer or recommendation based on the customer's profile and history.

Many companies use customer segmentation to make prospects and customers recognizable across an organization and all of its channels. Platinum, gold, and silver levels and loyalty programs are obvious customer recognition tags that can be used to designate and prepare treatments in each contact and channel.

Other forms of recognition include identifying not just the customer's current or future value, but also the customer's condition. Does the customer have an urgent need? Is the customer in danger with broken glass in packaging? Does the customer's livelihood depend on a good customer experience?

Customer service representatives are often trained to probe for these types of conditions to quickly identify and resolve a customer problem. Salespeople are trained to uncover the customer's decision criteria and situation in order to script a sales experience that raises the probability that a customer will buy.

Recognizing a customer in a contact in the CxC Matrix means that the customer's situation is taken into account to create the best outcome for the customer and the company.

Fulfill

Simply deliver what the customer expects in this contact—quickly and efficiently satisfy her needs based on her values, relationship to date, and channel capabilities.

While "Fulfill" seems simple and obvious, it is often difficult to achieve and most frustrating to the customer fixated on her single objective.

"What Ifs?" Quick Test

- If a customer calls and wants 100 units of your product immediately, how does your company respond?

- What if the customer goes to your website and wants to buy 100 units with cash right now? What would that experience look like?

Would he need to enter multiple single orders? Would he be billed and invoiced separately?

- What if a customer calls to cancel your service or return your product or if he tries to cancel or arrange a return online?

Most often, customers do not know the best solution, the best product configuration, or the best means to return a defective product. The CxC Matrix is meant to help expose the best available options at the customer's point of contact.

Upgrade

Each customer contact is an opportunity to strengthen the relationship. Each contact should seek to upgrade relationships to their next level. For example, invite customers to join a loyalty program and receive ongoing email, text, offers, news, and best practice communications. Encourage customers to join a frequent buyer program, automatic replenishment, or automatic renewing service program to protect their investments and make ongoing purchases and service easier.

Ask customers to buy in every contact. Encourage customers that call customer support to buy the latest and greatest product version to replace their obsolete product or service.

Cross-sell

Every contact should be evaluated for its ability to sell another product or service, either from your company or from a partner company. Companies should design propositions delivered through treatments that best fit the needs of the customer at each stage in each channel and continuously test what sells best and grows total customer lifetime value.

Expand

Each contact is a milestone that should strengthen, not weaken, the relationship. Expanding the relationship means expanding the customers' participation in the company network and community, encouraging them to use, access, experience, and buy other services.

A simple customer relationship expansion objective is to encourage customers to experience another channel: explore the web, visit a store, use a coupon from the web, or recruit customers to special events.

Loyalty programs, newsletter subscriptions, customer alert subscriptions, and events are all methods of expanding customer relationships and growing company and brand exposures.

Educate

Educate customers on your business, on your processes, and on how to better use your product, services, and resources for their benefit. Be the single source and primary conduit to best practices for your most valuable customers. Provide links to community websites, forums, and commentary.

Collect

Collect and store data from every customer contact, transaction, and interaction. Ideally, collect data about the quality of the contact and the customer's perceptions of how the contact was conducted. Record the data used to determine each treatment, the personal information, questions, answers, activities, and entities associated with each contact. Capture all of the elements and attributes associated with each contact in order to best understand the customer's experience and opportunities, as well as to improve the performance of future contacts.

"Do what you do so well that they will want to see it again and bring their friends."

—Walt Disney

Generate Referrals

Every contact should ask for referrals:

- Coupons for friends in an envelope.

- Offer emails with simple forwarding instructions.

- Invitations for friends and colleagues to attend social events.

- Asking customers on support calls if they know of anyone else who can use such a solution.

Message allocation from segmentation to syndication

Customize and Personalize Messages at the Right Cost-justifiable Level

Figure 7.1 Appropriate Targeting

It is common marketing sense to customize messages where you can do so efficiently. The tone, language, and benefits statement in a television advertisement or letter sent to the east coast of the United States will be different from a letter sent to the Midwest. Likewise, an offer for outsourced technology services sent to health care companies should be different from the same services offered to auto parts distributors. Different pictures and different language will raise the success of the marketing tactic.

You should strive to speak the customer's language as efficiently and cost-effectively as possible. Customers have been conditioned to reject offers, providers, and messages that do not target them appropriately.

Combine customer knowledge, technology, and creativity for customer-centric messages

Whether addressing an envelope with a person's familiar name or greeting a person in a store with "sir" or "madam," personalization or recognizing the individual helps you engage with customers at a deeper level. Personalization is used to create trust and confidence between the customer and your company, agent, and brand.

Customers expect to be recognized as repeat customers or as frequent visitors. "Being recognized" respects customers' investments in your company's brand and their previous buying process activities as they gather information, select services, learn more about offers, or call for support and assistance.

In the customer "Need, Shop, Buy" scenario, most of the messages contained in the slots are personalized using data the company collected from past purchases and contacts, plus personal data purchased from aggregators like Acxiom, Experian, Nielsen, Abacus, Dun & Bradstreet, and others. The CxC Matrix encourages you to leverage information about customer interests, income, lifestyle, family composition, finances, and other available information to enhance and model customers' values and preferences.

Additionally, you should use market and trade data combined with location, geography, and economic data to assess macro elements on customer performance. Internal information about locations, inventory, services, customer satisfaction, and Net Promoter Score, if available, should also be combined to provide a comprehensive composite of customer contact performance and potential.

Selecting messages from segmentation to monetization to syndication

Geographic Segmentation

"Dear Neighbor, the season is changing, it's time to . . ." Geographic segmentation broadcasts a single message to a geographic area, such as a country, region, state, or zip code. The container and its messages are the same for everyone in that geographic segment. This is used for high volume broad awareness campaigns and typically costs less per customer, although the overall expense can be higher due to the breadth of market coverage.

Demographic segmentation

"Dear Head of Household/New Homeowner . . ." Demographic segmentation typically uses personal information or regionally specific information to target customer messages. For example, if you want to reach highly affluent individuals you may send letters or buy names and phone numbers for residents of Park Avenue in New York City or all households in California zip codes where the average new home price is greater than $2 million.

"Congratulations on being in business for 5 years!" Business demographics are used to target businesses. Typically, marketers use industry type, Standards Industrial Classification Code (SIC Code), annual revenue, years in business, number of employees, and headquarters/branch locations.

Segmentation applications

Generally, 10 to 60 demographic variables are available to be used to select customers or append data to customer records. Appending data enables creative marketers to construct messages that more closely match a customer's ability to buy and buying preferences.

Targeted program execution

Marketing analysts also combine demographic variables to create more refined target groups, such as homeowners who purchased a house in the last 90 days and who also have one elementary school–aged child.

Behavioral Message Segmentation

"Dear Customer, about your purchase . . ." Behavioral segmentation uses information captured from prior customer contacts. Contacts may include purchases, website visits, phone inquiries, event registrations, general interest forms, service calls, upgrades, and other company or partner company contacts.

Behavioral information provides marketers with insights into the customer's interests, such as how, when, where, through which channel, and how often the customer contacts the company.

Armed with this information, creative marketers craft messages that align with customer interests and channel preferences.

Personalization

"Dear Miguel . . ." Personalization uses information from all available resources to craft a contact that strives to speak directly to a customer's needs, preferences, and circumstances, as if face-to-face. Some aspects of personalization that distinguish it from other forms of message targeting are the use of a customer's nickname, referencing current services, recent service and product use, or reference to other open issues that the customer is experiencing, such as abnormally

high frequency of calls or weather. Personalization requires your company to factor customer preferences into each contact and product use, such as offering process shortcuts for customers that have called before, registered before, or made identical purchases.

Personalization has evolved beyond putting the customer's name on an envelope, or greeting him by first name on the phone or nickname in an email, to include customer-specific contact, delivery, and assembly rules. Customers require companies to blend their best practices with prior customers with their own preferences and circumstances to ensure the best, most convenient, most productive, problem-free experience. Firms that fail to leverage customer information to personalize contacts and services will lose business and profit margin to companies that deliver greater perceived value to each customer based on the customer's defined terms.

Predictive Model Messaging

"Dear Miguel, a special offer just for you . . . " Predictive targeted messages use the results of the company's past contacts, combined with the customer's profile data, to predict what, when, and how much a customer is likely to buy. Predictive message targeting extends beyond who is likely to purchase a product and can be used to prompt messages to every customer contact point.

You can predict who will and will not buy which products at what price. You can also predict which customers are more likely to open an email, answer a phone, return a product, or buy a product. Additionally, you can predict which customers are least likely to pay for a product or pay full price and which ones are most likely to complain.

Your ability to predict how customers will respond contact-by-contact is dependent upon the amount of historic and ongoing activity data the company is able to capture. It also depends upon your company's modeling sophistication and messaging delivery system.

Your ability to act on its predictive modeling findings requires executive management commitment and sponsorship. It requires flexible and adaptive customer contact and operations systems, end-to-end customer demand-to-fulfillment-to-service chain visibility, and contact access points for execution.

Examples of ways to embed predictive models into core operations include:

- Web pages that use collaborative filtering to assemble messages.

- Call centers that queue and route calls to specially skilled agents, then prompt telemarketing scripts that dynamically change offers.

- Pick, pack, and ship automated packing systems that use business rules to insert various sales materials, product samples, and labels in distribution.

Commercialization

"Your message here . . . " In addition to segmenting messages for your own products and services, your company can sell your message slots to third parties. An offer for a barbecue grill might fall out of a monthly billing statement, or an offer for a magazine subscription or sweepstakes entry might come at the end of a customer service call.

You can commercialize a slot as easily as charging a third party for the privilege of putting a label on a box containing an advertising message. Here is an example: "Got Milk?" stickers on oranges or "Got Oranges?" stickers on milk cartons.

The concept of commercialization is an excellent way to grasp monetizing each contact's message slots. Ask, "Who would place a message here and for how much?" Exposing all of your contacts and slots and examining the current slot allocation, used and unused, is the catalyst for discussion among employees regarding valuing slots and contacts based on internally competing departments, products, and messages. Multi-product companies can choose to feature another division's products in their messages and charge the internal client for the opportunity. Likewise, you should identify which business partners may want to pay for the privilege of featuring their messages in an available slot and how much they would pay.

Affiliation

"Customers like you also like . . . " Affiliation message targeting takes commercialization to another level to blend two or more brands. It also links some back-end operations to create a seamless and continuous customer experience. Some commonplace examples of affiliate message delivery include payment options at a store or checkout page on a website, delivery options where the customer can select from a number of carriers at various price points, or cell phone replacement insurance options at contact signing. All of these services are provided by third parties but embedded in the core offering to be both convenient and transparent to the end customer.

The affiliate message delivery model is typically priced and managed as a gain-share model where parties agree on specific shared service, resource, integration, and process responsibilities. Both parties share in the revenue or profit generated from the success of the messages.

Syndication

"What would Google do?" Syndication is the most advanced form of message targeting. You can expose a message slot to a group of companies, stakeholders, or the open market in order for all parties to bid for the right to place their message in the slot.

The syndication model is most familiar in the online media market and web channels where message slots alongside news and information content are sold to the highest bidder.

Constantly updated through testing, web page technologies swap ads through a network of buyers and sellers at an enormous rate and with speed, flexibility, and tracking. As a result, companies have much more information on existing, registered, and repeat customers, along with the power of their brand and the equity built in their relationship (trust like Amazon, brand affiliation like Tiffany, American Express, Bank of America, or Goldman Sachs).

As you begin to realize the breadth and potential value of your contact network, and as messages continue to become digitized and network connected, more of them will be shared among businesses delivering complimentary and opportunistic products and services.

CHAPTER 8

The Customer Schematic

CxC Matrix DIY* (Do It Yourself)

You should be able to complete your own customer, department, and systems Matrix with the complete set of customer stages and channel categories in a short time, measured in hours rather than days and weeks. With a top level Matrix filled in, selected areas can be completed with greater detail based on your company's objectives.

*Caution: Use only enough detail to achieve an objective.

The Matrix diagram depicts your business's current customer infrastructure, along with the people, systems, and departments responsible for customer-facing operations, as well as all non-customer-facing operations responsible for designing, building, delivering, pricing, promoting, and supporting your company's products and services.

Five quick steps to building your company's CxC Matrix

Visualize: Inventory all customer contact points and respective systems.

Analyze: Count customers and observe customer flow.

Monetize: Assign dollar value to each customer.

Prioritize: Target focus areas based on strategic value, monetized opportunities, and risks.

Optimize: Set and monitor goals per contact point; allocate investments to best performing tactics and treatments; continuously improve process-based performance,

CxC Matrix development tips

You need to establish your own channel categories and stages in the consumer cycle. Modify the templates provided in this book to use terms familiar to your industry and, specifically, to your company (template downloads are available at *www.CustomerWorthy.com*).

> Channel categories are most important for strategy, market assessment, and planning, while individual contact channel assignment is critical for financial analysis and contact design. As you insert more detail beneath the channel category level, the Matrix becomes more valuable as a tool for specific functions, activities, and tactics. Details relating to systems and functionality help business units and information technology departments engage in a dialog about needs, requirements, and technical specifications. Details regarding media, containers, slots, and messages provide a platform for describing and managing the dialog in each customer contact. Activity costs and projected revenue details are important for finance planning and department managers. Later chapters will provide more information for each department or function.

What is most important is that each channel and contact be listed only once in the Matrix to maintain the mutual exclusivity of the channel and stage cells.

Step 1. Visualize—
Inventory All Customer Contact Points and Respective Systems

When introducing the preliminary Matrix concepts, it is best to start with broad categories of customer contact channels using familiar terms that your employees recognize such as inbound phone, outbound phone, customer support, infield sales, office locations, partner resellers, direct mail, geographies (i.e., markets, territories, regions).

It is also best to start with the most familiar and obvious channels grouped by categories and then insert major missing channel categories.

For example, your company may not use resellers or partners to distribute your product, but you should list third parties as a channel category because your customers are likely to try to fulfill their needs in all channels. A large number of customers may search for your products and services in channels that your company is not using or where you are under-represented and under-invested.

It is important to address Matrix stages discreetly by interaction channel, as customers have different expectations based on channel.

However, it isn't necessary to complete the entire grid. You may not take orders online, or you may provide a service that you do not believe can be categorized as "accepted" or "delivered." These types of adjustments are not required at this level of analysis.

Quick Picture: For a strategic review and to quickly kick off the "Think Like a Customer" discussion:

Figure 8.1 CxC Matrix

	1. Awareness	2. Information	3. Identification	4. Selection	5. Negotiation	6. Contract	7. Logistics	8. Delivery	9. Acceptance	10. $ Collection	11. Use	12. Care/Support	13. Repair	14. Disposal	15. Community
Geography															
Digital															
Location															
Third party															
One-on-one															
Community															

Step 2. Analyze—
Count Customers and Observe Customer Flow

Put your customers in the Matrix, and examine customer flow and bottlenecks. Identify how many unique customers exist at each contact point or cell for a specific unit of time. These numbers do not have to be precise. Best guesses work fine in order to expedite the next level of findings.

Establish a timeframe for collecting customer count data, as different systems and business types have varying data capture and access capabilities. It is best to start with annual customer counts per contact and stage since annual counts should be the easiest and fastest to collect. Where available, monthly counts should be a near-term goal as month-to-month data reflects customer flow performance.

Get the Easiest Data Using the Quickest Means

Managers should not get bogged down at this stage with an exact number of customers, nor should they be concerned with anonymous versus identified customers just yet. Anonymous customers are those with contacts that do not require identification or recognition, such as a website visit, a call into a call center, or a visit to a store. Estimates for total number of customers per contact channel and stage should be completed as quickly as possible.

Each channel is supported by a corresponding system. For example, boxes filled in the warehouse should be classified as "8. Delivery" stage under the "one-on-one" channel. Fill in the number of customers who were sent shipments on a monthly basis. Here are some examples of quick counts by channel, by stage: How many website visits, incoming service calls, partner sales calls, web mentions, newspaper mentions, returned items, in-field sales calls?

This simple analysis exposes strategic questions regarding the use of entire channels such as Internet, third parties, or direct sales, while typically uncovering bottlenecks in customer demand processes and customer service capabilities or resources.

Analyze Deliverables

- Metrics, performance benchmarks
- Return on investment (ROI) scenario framework and components
- "What if" system and process design scenario framework
- CxC Matrix goal setting and coaching framework
- Strategic SWAT (Strength, Weakness, Actions, Tactics) analysis framework
- Preliminary integration or overlay with other management performance frameworks, metrics, and methods

Other Matrix Contact Point Analysis Areas

1. Define nature of the intra-process links.

2. Audit each contact's function and capabilities. Develop an understanding of the capacities and time lags associated with each business process.

3. Sample Questions and Observations:

    - Look at the total numbers at the bottom of each column. Columns 1-8 depict the conversion rate from life stage to life stage which, when combined with monetization, can be used to quantify the value of any resource investment.

    - For each high potential channel, look further at the channel details, and discuss opportunities and risks associated with making changes by channel, by consumer cycle.

    - This Matrix should provide a quick quantifiable view of multi-channel customer behavior. While this is a macro view of performance across stages, management should discuss the interrelationship of web to location customers, third party to web to location customers, etc., and the existing contact network's fitness and ability to meet customer needs. Do the current structures and resources meet evolving customer needs?

- Highlight the experience stages by channel that are most critical to your business success over the next 6-12 months.

95%: The percentage of retail companies that think it's valuable to use data to project customer lifetime value.

35%: The percentage that actually do it.

—Retail Systems Research, Benchmark Study, July 2007

Step 3. Monetize—
Assign Dollar Value to Each Customer

Insert estimated annual revenue per customer. Multiply the value per customer times the number of customers in each cell. Summarize the stage numbers in each column.

> **Note on Double-Counting:** At this point, the raw numbers summed in each column represent double and triple-counted customers, as most companies cannot discreetly track individual customers from channel to channel, contact to contact, and stage to stage in the consumer cycle. While getting to the point that individuals are distinguishable in each cell is an excellent long-term goal, precision down to the customer level is not necessary now.

Lifetime Value or Annual Revenue per Customer

How much is each customer worth over his entire relationship? If you do not have a lifetime value figure, or lifetime value is considered unreliable, use annual revenue per customer to assess the potential value of each cell. For most companies, it is worthwhile to use annual revenue per customer or per product line to illustrate and visualize value pockets. Another monetization alternative is to create a separate Matrix using each department's customer value number and for your entire company to come to an agreement on which number fits best.

Managers can now quickly rank the areas that represent the greatest opportunity for revenue enhancement and cost reduction by placing monetary values at each channel, customer stage, and contact. Simply put: "How many customers will be affected with what revenue gain or cost reduction?"

If your company is a multi-line business that markets to a diverse customer population across countries and markets, you may want to complete CxC Matrices for each logical division of your business.

Figure 8.2 CxC Matrix

	1. Awareness	2. Information	3. Identification	4. Selection	5. Negotiation	6. Contract	7. Logistics	8. Delivery	9. Acceptance	10. $ Collection	11. Use	12. Care/Support	13. Repair	14. Disposal	15. Community
Geography															
Digital															
Location															
Third party															
One-on-one															
Community															
Monthly flow	10%	10%	10%	10%	10%	10%	10%	10%	10%	10%	10%	10%	10%	10%	
Opportunity	$	$	$	$	$	$	$	$	$	$	$	$	$	$	$

Step 4. Prioritize—

Target Areas Based on Their Strategic Value, Monetized Opportunities, and Risks

Target the Matrix contact points that have the greatest strategic and monetary importance. Use the Matrix to connect contact points and activities to specific corporate objectives. Then, complete the Matrix to include goals, actions, owners, and systems to ensure execution excellence.

Prioritize areas with the greatest benefit:

- **Most vulnerable**—cost leakage, competitive threats, market misalignment

- **Opportunistic**—high growth, quick, simple changes required

- **Competitive threat assessment**—channel coverage, service configurations, service quality, sophistication, perceived preferential value margin assessment

- **Enormous opportunity**—land grab, strategic opportunity design, test market simulations, new market entry, merger, acquisition, expansion, and consolidation scenarios

- **The Hot Spot Method**—CxC Matrix hot spots: biggest gains and biggest costs cells direct focus to areas for immediate performance lifts

Focus on one area at a time, and complete the Matrix details for each target contact point. Realize that contacts are related via customer path and internally shared systems and processes, which may require bridging resources and joint department planning.

Step 5. Optimize—
Set and Monitor Goals per Contact Point

At this point, the Matrix provides a static view of a company's business, depicting how many customers contact the company, its brand, its products, partners, and messages across each channel and at each stage on a periodic basis—monthly or annually.

You should be able to get to this step and have a CxC Matrix view of your business in 1 to 12 weeks.

You derive tremendous value and uncover "quick wins" (high return on investment with a short payback window and little to no capital expenditures or out-of-pocket costs) just from the discussions, departmental exchanges and discoveries that take place while building this static, point-in-time customer view.

However, you should not lose sight of the ultimate goal of building a customer worthy mindset among managers. The CxC Matrix provides a system of sensors across your entire customer contact network to help you immediately and knowledgeably execute every customer contact optimally.

Flow: The Challenge

Customer flow to revenue stages (Stages 1–6) and through cost stages (7–15) is the single metric that every manager should monitor. Answer these simple questions:

- At what rate are new customers appearing?
- At what rate are customers buying?
- At what rate are customers repeat buying?
- At what rate do customers require service and care?

These simple questions require managers to track the length of time customers spend at each stage and specific customer movement from stage to stage and channel to channel. Again, not all channels and stages need to be completely transparent and accessible on day one, but those channels and contact areas deemed critical in the earlier stages should be closely monitored as soon as possible.

In summary, set performance goals by department and contact owner that are visible across the company. Use existing measurement and reporting systems to report on customer performance by channel and stage, making every effort to integrate with current performance measures.

CxC Matrix Reporting—Alerts and Alarms

Your reporting should be set up to alert management to anomalies. For example:

- A spike in customers requesting information.

- A drop-off in website customers buying (moving from Stage 5 to Stage 6).
- An increase in time for all customers moving from Stage 2 to Stage 6.

Each of these, detected by alarms set off by changes in benchmark performance, are indications of business risk or opportunity. These changes may be due to obvious activities, such as a new advertising program or a mention of a product on a national news broadcast. Or they may be due to less obvious activities or market events like a competitor's new product launch or price change, bad weather during a peak sale weekend, or inventory outages at a primary distribution point. Transparency to changes in customer flow provides early warnings to downstream managers, finance, executive management, and shareholders. This is important because changes in customer flow directly affect revenue, costs, and income.

Continuously encourage employees to innovate and contribute customer growth and cost containment suggestions. Establish recognition and reward systems based on customer performance for every department tied to and directly traceable to customer performance observable in the CxC Matrix.

CHAPTER 9

The Customer's Network

Count the contacts

Jose heads to lunch at the Panera across the highway from his office. While he is deciding between six types of bread and 30 combinations of top-pings for his ham and cheese sandwich, the lunch shop's 42-inch flat screen plays a series of in-house commercials to the right of the large illuminated menu board. Above and left, another screen tuned to CNN features a doc-tor being interviewed about eating a healthy diet, followed by a Subway commercial.

Seemingly oblivious to all of this chatter, Jose is now fourth in line to order but becomes distracted by his Google phone vibrating in his pocket. He checks the "alert" to see who is trying to reach him and sees an email message from online electronics retailer Tiger Direct announcing a "three-hour sale on 26-inch combination personal computer and high-definition digital television monitors for $99."

Still waiting in line, Jose clicks the link to the Tiger Direct website on his phone, and after three more clicks, he has logged in to his corporate Tiger Direct account. He changes the quantity on the pre-completed order page to "6" and clicks "submit" to complete his order. His three-inch phone screen displays "order completed" along with a confirmation code and a shipment notification message verifying that the monitors will arrive at his office in two days.

Jose looks up at the cashier and orders his sandwich, adding a cinnamon roll as a reward for saving his company more than $400. He deserves it. Four minutes later, he leaves the store with his lunch and passes a big brand electronics retailer advertising a "just reduced 22-inch monitor for $209" with the notation, "only 3 left." Jose shakes his head and murmurs quietly, "They just don't get it."

The bottom line is that customers have figured out the system, and they are motivated by price, urgency, quality, trust, and ease of doing business.

The customer's network

Tiger Direct participates in Jose's network. The customer, Jose, gladly lets Tiger Direct interrupt his personal lunch hour not just to offer him something free, but also to sell him something.

Jose designs his network to carefully meet his needs by selecting who has access to his email accounts, phone numbers, addresses, and devices. His criteria are personal, and they change as his needs change. He chooses some for convenience and others out of necessity, like his bank accounts and credit cards. He chooses still others for curiosity and entertainment. But, most importantly, Jose is in control of who is "in" and who is "out," the times of day that he is open to messages, and the types and frequency of the messages, offers, updates, and alerts.

In the customer's network—phone, email, car, game device, television— information moves from one device to another according to the customer's preferences. The customers use "rules" to orchestrate information around their network.

Thanks to pervasive access to the Internet and the reach of handheld computer and communication devices, customers blur the division between personal life and work life, personal time and work time. This also changes customer perceptions and expectations for how things should operate regarding business dialogue, information access, process portability and mobility, feedback, and assistance at each contact.

Your customers are on duty nearly 24/7, armed with Blackberries, iPhones, other smart phones, and tablet and ultraportable data retrieving and communication devices. Your customer's network transcends the traditional barriers of work time, personal time, and leisure time, creating a digital composite persona that persists across devices, websites, calendars, channels, locations, activities, transactions, and messages.

Companies must learn to "Think Like a Customer!"

"We don't decide how long the people are in the store. What we decide is how easy it is for you within the 21 minutes you've allocated to get what you want."

— Stephen Quinn, Walmart Marketing Chief

The hyper-aware customer knows more about your company, your product, and your service than any individual he is likely to come into contact with during the entire buying process.

Customers have breached the wall at most companies. Information is everywhere: embedded customers, embedded analysts, and embedded competitors. Review sites are springing up, submitting unsolicited reviews of your products and services at a host of websites. People blog, instant message, Tweet, broadcast, and narrowcast about how wonderful or how horrible you are.

Digitization Enables Transparency

Past, current, and potential customers, as well as competitors, partners, and employees participate in message networks and communities that share information about your business. All parties freely discuss pricing, quality, activities, affiliations, upcoming developments, customer satisfaction, corporate shenanigans—just about everything.

If someone wants to find out more information that isn't currently available, he can simply go to a post, build his own blog, or go to an industry website. He can submit a question or opinion to a bulletin board and wait for commentary to come back. To add to management's frustration, most of the information is exchanged anonymously without any way of verifying or tracking who leaked what or who made up the story.

Again, the Internet and the age of digitalization have changed the corporate information landscape forever. A company's operations, lawsuits, and board member activities—significant or insignificant, real or unreal—are equally searchable and accessible to anyone with an interest.

In order to compete, your company must seek an invitation to your customer networks. You may become the source and destination for all related information, or you may link customers to the most convenient source. If you cannot be the source, find a way to get on customer maps and radar, even if it means participating in commentary and services not specifically related to your product or service. Provide a means to get customers what they need. This is how you create repeat business and the eventual revenue payoff.

The answer is in the Matrix

Do not make the mistake of assuming that customers know how to design products. They don't. But observing how customers get, find, use, and link your service to their needs will uncover areas where your business can create innovative products, services, features, and partnerships.

The Next Big Thing

The next great breakthrough will not be a brand new service. It will be a combination of products, services, features, and functions that closely wrap themselves around the customer's need-set and adapt to the customer's life stage. An example might be a bundle of financial services that adapt to a customer's age, family attributes, transaction behavior, and season using best practices for balancing savings, spending, investing, and insurance. The Matrix enables customers to benefit from this information that is automatically built in to their service and applied to their specific situation.

The customer is the true arbiter of good corporate decisions

Try to think like a customer. Your customers make the same cost or expense-based decisions as your company. So, every "go forward" decision in the CxC Matrix process involves a minimum of two parties balancing trade-offs and exchanging value.

Consumers weigh value based on their own value sets. Convenience, proximity, brand, product fit, total cost of ownership, and quality of service are estimated by the shopper who builds a checklist that establishes a set of expectations for vendors, sellers, and servicers. Shoppers and customers have become more aware of their purchase options, so they leverage the Matrix process transparency to negotiate demands at every stage.

Buyers and sellers knowingly monitor their investment and expenses throughout the buying process, weighing trade-offs at each stage:

- "Buy now or delay?"
- "Customize product and wait or take available product immediately?"
- "Use vendor's financing or alternative funding sources?"
- "Buy or lease?"

All parties involved in the customer experience process have a vested interest in each contact. What has changed is that, up until now, companies have only looked at their internal expenses where they have some degree of control. Now, companies are forced to acknowledge the customer's investment and stated or implied specifications and requirements. Perhaps even more troublesome is the fact that this entire experience may be observed, critiqued, mocked, or mimicked in the transparent marketplace where service contacts are recorded and exposed on websites and forums like YouTube, Facebook, Twitter, and CNet.

However, there is a great opportunity in all of this. By understanding and addressing the customer's expectations and expenses in every contact, you can expose greater revenue and cost savings opportunities for both parties. These opportunities exist in nearly every customer interaction and contact, whether the contact is person-to-person, or person-to-machine. It happens during the purchasing cycle, the buying transaction, and in each stage of the customer experience.

"BlueLight spokesman Dave Karraker said the slowdowns on his company's site were caused in part because of customers who were using shopping bots to find PlayStation 2 game consoles. In recent days, BlueLight has been able to redirect traffic from those bots, and sales have been increasing 5 percent per day, Karraker said."

—"E-tail Sites Resilient Amid Latest Holiday Hubbub,"
Troy Wolverton, CNET News

The rise of the professional customer

Customers get it. Not only have they mastered how to buy from you and are likely to share this knowledge, but many buyers are also becoming sellers in secondary markets. And if they are not selling your products and services, they are still likely to influence the market at review sites, blogs, and industry forums.

If you have not done so already, log onto the websites on the following list, and enter your company name and one of your specific product names. Even try one of your own product identification codes, and see what pops up. Many managers are surprised to see that their products and services are posted on other sites for resale. Products and services are typically sold as after-market items in used or repaired condition or they are rebranded.

- eBay
- Craigslist
- Amazon
- Google

Managers should walk through the entire customer experience provided by these sites to get a customer's view of what he finds as he researches your products, services, and company.

Do not betray trust—build value!

What if my car sent a message to a service station that I needed oil, and the car negotiated the price along my daily route? Why not have a program that optimizes prices for my commonly purchased items along my regular commuting route? But let's not stop there! Why not have a "buy" button that assembles purchased products without my having to stop, so I only have to pick them up later from a single location on my return trip. This implies a great level of mutual trust between buyers and sellers, but similar models exist where customers have professional buyers, use concierge services, and buy through aggregators like Amazon. With a growing level of distrust of companies that handle our personal data, new service configurations are likely to evolve that balance privacy and convenience to benefit both the company and the customer.

"Give trust, and you'll get it double in return."

—Kees Kamies, *production manager in a facility that employed socially and mentally disabled persons*

CHAPTER 10

Start the Revolution

The revolution begins the next time your customer is on hold—when his time and patience starts to waste away and he begins to speculate, "There must be a better way."

The revolution starts when your customer listens to the unintelligible voice mail that your company left. It starts when someone at your company defers a decision for a customer. Your customers may jot a note on a blog or a forum. They may Tweet on Twitter or tag comments on another social networking website. They may even start a free website or turn on their web cam to record their idle thoughts and vent.

"Casey Neistat, 24, is one consumer who took his case to cyberspace when his iPod died in September 2003 and he discovered Apple didn't offer a replacement battery. "They suggested I buy a new iPod," Neistat says. Instead, he and brother Van Neistat, 29—both professional filmmakers—made a short video including Casey's phone conversation with an Apple customer service representative. They posted it at iPodsdirtysecret.com and emailed 40 friends about the site, which has now received more than 1.5 million hits. "We had no idea [the site] would get the attention it did," Casey says. (Apple, by the way, now has a battery replacement program for the iPod). All the rage: angry consumers are using the Internet to get revenge. How can you keep them happy?"

—Chris Penttila in *Entrepreneur*

While he is online, on hold, or waiting for the technician to arrive, there are communities of other customers like him online, on hold, idly waiting, and at some stage of frustration. The issue for you is how to make the best use of the customers' time or how to create some equitable system for compensating customers for their time and effort invested. What are the options? Reschedule? Make an offer to credit $5 if you call back again in two hours? Offer an MP3 ringtone (yes, introduce a new service), offer a gift card from a partner company? Apologize?

The bottom line? An idle customer is a dangerous customer.

It is customer payback time!

Figure 10.1

```
COMPANY NAME                                    DATE : _____
STREET
CITY, STATE, ZIP
                OWES: YOUR NAME HERE      $ _____.___
_____ DOLLARS FOR _____ HOURS

CUSTOMERPAYBACK.COM
```

It's time for businesses to compensate customers for the time they waste.

CustomerPayback monetizes customer relationships from the customer's perspective. A customer simply enters the business name, the amount of his time wasted, and a fair customer wage per hour at CustomerPayback. Customers may choose to provide more details about their grievances, the company's errors, additional damages, suggested solutions, and tips for other customers to avoid problems. CustomerPayback's ultimate goal is customer experience improvement.

The site calculates the dollar equivalent of the time the customer invested in the company and creates a receipt. This receipt is then sent to the offending company and recorded and reported in the CustomerPayback website.

Monetizing the customer time that companies waste should bring attention to the greatest business offenders, while also providing a means for customers to suggest to companies how they can improve their processes.

CustomerPayback creates a dialogue between customers and businesses in order to help companies like yours resolve systemic problems and identify, monetize, analyze, and repair customer complaints as a result of broken customer processes.

The site also highlights worst offending companies, as well as featuring news about companies that are rectifying issues and making customer time a priority.

CustomerPayback recommends that your business respond to customer complaints and solution suggestions, which should also help you meet some of the service shortfalls listed in the National Customer Rage Study. Note that five of the top six "remedies" are non-monetary in nature:

1. An explanation of why the problem occurred (69%)
2. Assurance the problem would not be repeated (69%)
3. Product/service fixed (67%).
4. A "thank you for my business" (67%)
5. An apology (54%)
6. Opportunity to vent (54%)
7. Money back (43%)
8. Free product/service in the future (35%)
9. Compensation for lost time/inconvenience (22%)
10. Revenge (12%)

Source: Used with permission from CCA Office of the Ombudsman, 2005 National Customer Rage Study, www.ombudsman.ed.gov, fsaombudsmanoffice@ed.gov, Editor, Mike Turpenoff.

The Customer Rage Study brings something else to the attention of managers and customers. Most of us would agree that we are most frustrated when companies disregard and under-appreciate our time. The Rage study reported that customers listed their most common "damages suffered" as "loss of time" and "loss of money."

CustomerPayback maintains a database by company of the amount of hours and dollars each company owes its customers. This site also encourages businesses to contact customers directly, offer coupons, cash, charitable donations, or some form of community service to help mend their customer relationships.

More confessions (continued from the Preface)

Confession 2: I have been on both sides of every contact intersection in the CxC Matrix. I have been to the other side. I have worked in the multi-thousand cube call centers where hard-working, dedicated customer service representatives show up every day, 24 hours a day to answer calls, online chats, emails, and letters from angry, frustrated, and generally unhappy customers. They handle problems that they had no part in causing for companies they don't directly work for.

I worked at Macy's in the mall the day after Christmas, where I greeted customers who arrived extra early to wait in long lines in order to argue the "refund price without a receipt policy." (Yes, that was me who caught the sweater and box thrown by the person fourth in line from the register as she shouted, "*$#/¢! you and *$#/¢! Macy's!" And thank yous to all of the people in line who apologized for the enraged customer and cheered as she left).

I have walked through the warehouses and shipping rooms where millions of letters and boxes are stuffed, labeled, and sent to your door. Likewise, I have spent time in the returns room where defective, mislabeled, and returned items appear by the truckload.

Confession 3: I am a salesperson, and I believe that in this new age where businesses and customers are so tightly connected we are all in sales.

I have written advertisements for radio, television, direct mail, websites, point of purchase, and billboards designed to intentionally and measurably raise customer expectations and make splendid promises enticing customers to "act now!"

Confession 4: I handled your data—without malfeasance—to help companies build better solutions for you and to gain better understanding of your needs and interests while trying to extract your optimum potential revenue.

Confession 5: I don't mind being on hold. Make "hold time" informational and/or entertaining.

There is a better way, and it is not that hard

Customer satisfaction scores do not need to continue to decline. Your technology, marketing and cost of sale do not need to escalate to chase every possible deal and one-up your competitor in every channel in every contact. This book is intended to help you avoid these kinds of problems by aligning your company's business objectives with its customer's interests, values, and expectations, making every contact customer worthy. Its goal is to help you improve relationships with customers by not wasting customer time, money, or attention. It is designed to simply make it more pleasurable to do business with you.

You should be angry, too

We are all customers at work, at home, in restaurants, on vacation, while grocery shopping, surfing the web, at the DMV, while filing our taxes, and so on. This is why this customer worthiness is so important. We are all victims of the same unsatisfactory customer experiences, and each of us holds part of the solution.

The Customer Worthy MBA

You should traverse your own company's CxC Matrix and have every manager in your company do the same. You should go through the same process at your major competitors to get your competitors' customer experience. At a minimum, this should be performed on an annual basis and should also be conducted any time there is a major market or competitor shift, merger, major event in your industry, new product launch, or news event.

For a blank, full-size printable pdf version of the CxC Matrix go to: www.customerworthy.com

25 Customer experiences to make you a better manager

For each of these experiences, keep a journal, taking notes about every contact, stage, and channel.

1. Send a letter to your bank asking for an explanation of the interest calculation on your money market checking account. Ask, "How much will $10,000 be worth after two years?" Send an email asking the same question.

2. Send a letter, email, and phone your wireless provider asking how to lower your monthly bill and get better service.

3. Write a letter to your energy company (gas or electricity) asking it to please lower your monthly bill.

4. Send flowers to yourself from 1-800-flowers.com and FTD.com. Note the differences in each stage in each channel using the Matrix.

5. Subscribe to WineLibrary. Buy two bottles, and return one. (Enjoy the other.)

6. Write and submit a product review on Amazon.

7. Join LinkedIn, and write a recommendation for 2 coworkers.

8. Open a Facebook, Twitter, Myspace, and Google account. Then cancel each account.

9. Go on a car scavenger hunt, shopping at: Mercedes, Lexus, Mini Cooper, Ford, Cars.com, and Edmunds. First, shop online for a vehicle in the same size and color as what you currently drive. Then, visit each dealership, take a test drive, and get the lowest price.

10. Shop for a copy of Microsoft Office software online, and try to get the best price and the shortest delivery time. Bonus points for using online chat. Note the delivery cost, shipping cost, taxes, and version variations.

11. Visit, register, and join Gevalia Coffee Club. After you get the free coffee stuff, quit, and keep track of your email and mail offers/follow-up. Try to do the same thing at Starbucks online.

12. Sell something on eBay, buy something on eBay, and bid for something and win it on eBay.

13. Set up and use Google Adwords for two months.

14. Make and post a YouTube video. Send the link to three people you know.

15. Become a Microsoft partner. Complete the form at https://partner. microsoft.com.

16. Become a Salesforce Partner at https://www.salesforce.com/partners/apply-partners.jsp.

17. Become an Oracle Partner at http://www.oracle.com/index.html.

18. Become a WebTrends Reseller at https://www.webtrends.com/Partners/AuthorizedResellers/ResellerApplication.aspx.

19. Host a gathering for people you don't know using LinkedIn and/or a temporary Google website. Offer to buy appetizers for the event, come up with a subject, follow up with a thank you, post pictures and video on Facebook and YouTube, and link to your invite web page.

20. Go to your local Department of Motor Vehicles for one hour when they open. Then, go to the local library and Starbucks. Then, return to the DMV.

21. Sponsor a child at WorldVision.

22. Shop for a trip to Orlando using Travelocity, Priceline (name your

own price—$25, really!), Hotels.com, HomeAway, Expedia, and VRBO.

23. Then, go to Orlando and visit Disney World, Universal Studios, Sea World, and Gator World. For a bonus, take someone in a wheelchair to add perspective.

24. Spend eight hours shopping on New York's Fifth Avenue, three hours in the Short Hills Mall in Short Hills, New Jersey, 30 minutes at Costco, 30 minutes at Walmart, 30 minutes at PETCO, and 30 minutes at Staples. Join the loyalty program for each one online after your visit.

25. Write a press release, and post it at www.openpr.com/news/submit.html or some other free press release website.

CHAPTER 11

Customer Privacy Is Nothing to Kid About

Satellites watch your house, your office, and your children's school. Traffic cameras follow your daily commute turn by turn. Software watches where you surf on the web, tracks your eyeball's movement across pages, and calculates each click, pause, and impulse. This software predicts where you will go next and guesses your interests by popping up images and offers to tempt you to act now.

"New gadgets installed in cars will be able to tell insurers how many miles drivers have logged, what times of the day they drive, and even how frequently they abruptly stop and start. Other incarnations of the technology involve GPS devices that can even tell insurers precisely where drivers have traveled, and if they obeyed local speed limits."

—Red Tape Chronicles, http://redtape.cnbc.com

Even your car spies on you with its GPS (your phone may be an accomplice, too, as are other devices in your home and office). Your movements, each tenth of a mile, are measured. In-car computers log each press on the accelerator and brake, speed, and condition. E-ZPass, parking meters, gas purchases with credit cards, and loyalty cards all generate mile markers detailing your customer journey.

In the background and around the world, unbeknownst to you, third parties harvest this information, enhancing it with the other information they have gathered, modeled, and scored. Information about you is packaged, and your digital persona is sold to the highest bidder. Worse yet, it is sold as often as possible to anyone who will pay. Your information, your interests, and where you spend your time is packaged and sold by local, national, and global vendors.

So, what does this mean to business owners?

How much is my data worth anyway?

The two stories that follow shed some light on customer data breaches and customer identity theft. The stories are not related and Story #1 is an illustrative account told by security experts to depict standard operations in identity theft rings. They highlight why companies of all sizes and across all industries must require more stringent customer information handling processes. The most shocking aspect of these stories, which are just two among thousands, is how simple and easy it is for the thieves in each scenario to steal customer data.

What the stories do not show, of course, is the pain, annoyance, time, effort, and suffering that each of the customers went through to reverse the transactions, adjust their accounts, and repair their credit. The total cost of these crimes is many times what the thieves actually stole.

Story #1

June 24, 2008, Bangalore: Chandri receives a message back from "RBL Ventures," asking him to show them a sample of 100 transactions so that they can evaluate the data. Four hours later, they email him back, offering $12 per usable card. He emails half the data. RBL responds an hour later, saying that there is usable data on 42,174 valid, separate cards. They offer to pay him $506,088 for those cards and will wire the funds to his bank account. He emails them his bank account information.

June 24, 2008, Bucharest: Elescieu gets the first 50,000 credit card transactions from "Reliable Supplier" and runs the numbers through a program that spots duplicates and weeds out cards known to have expired or been cancelled. He subtracts another 2,000 for good measure and offers $12 to a seller he thinks is inexperienced.

June 25, 2008, Bangalore: Having confirmed that the funds are in his bank account, Chandri sends the other 500,000 transactions and gets a wire transfer for $464,088 for 38,674 cards.

June 28, 2008, Bucharest: Elescieu takes the credit card data to an associate who manufactures counterfeit credit cards.

July 12, 2008, Bangalore: Chandri buys a new car for cash, and takes his family shopping. He invests the money in bank CDs.

July 14, 2008, Bucharest: Elescieu distributes the counterfeit cards to a ring of associates who will use them quickly, primarily to buy high ticket items that can be resold for cash. He gets a cut of the cash they raise in return for his promise to provide more counterfeit cards in the future.

July 28, 2008, Moultrie: Morgan gets her credit card statement in the mail and finds $4,326 in charges for purchases of consumer electronics and jewelry in several European cities. She immediately calls her credit card issuer and reports the fraudulent transactions to a customer service representative, who cancels the card and tells Morgan that she need only pay for the purchases she made. Her new card will be mailed to her in a few days."

> —*Transaction Trends*, December Data Security Investigations, "Anatomy of Two Breach Scenarios with Two Very Different Outcomes" by Richard H. Gamble, *gamble10@earthlink.net*

Story #2

"Illegitimate customers are placing orders for flowers using stolen credit card information. The orders are typically placed via fax, email, and/or hearing-impaired relay calls. The perpetrator then requests that the florists wrap the flower arrangements in various amounts of cash and bill the difference to the credit card number(s) provided. These orders have been known to reach $4,000. A shipping address for the order is then provided to the merchant.

In some instances, the perpetrators have been known to hire an unsuspecting accomplice to pick up the flowers in person. This accomplice is then instructed to ship the flowers via UPS or the mail.

When the true cardholder receives the floral charge on their monthly statement, they will initiate a chargeback, as the order was placed without their authorization. As a result, the merchant will become liable for the fraudulent sale."

—"Visa Alerts of Floral Credit Card Fraud,"
www.merchantaccountalerts.com

The florist story above is especially galling since it appears that the employees at the florist are going out of their way to meet a customer's needs by wrapping cash in the bouquet.

Missing pieces—just a calculable piece of the puzzle

Businesses have to think like a customer and be aware of how easily customer data can be stolen, manipulated and fraudulently manufactured and used. The CxC Matrix depicts how the missing pieces of a customer's digital mosaic are easily filled in using predictive models and algorithms. Simply put, customers are not that unique. Consumption and purchase patterns, delivery and payment preferences follow similar paths that make differentiating real behaviors from manufactured or simulated behavior near impossible to distinguish. As more channels become digitized and web connected, customer activities will become even more transparent and more easily simulated. More data constantly becomes available as digital television and radio behavior is captured per click. Favorites on both are readily available. As customers unknowingly link members of their households, their social networks, their work relationships, digital identities will become more vulnerable to poaching, phishing, eavesdropping, fraud and theft.

So, what do your customers do? Stop using credit cards? Disconnect their internet connections, GPS, satellite radio and cable television? Stop traveling for business? Not likely. Yet, regardless of what they might think or how they might try, customers are not that unique, and they likely make the majority of their purchases locally within four miles or 15 minutes of their homes and workplaces. The digital breadcrumbs from census data, surveys they completed, loan applications, health club and group membership applications, health records, sweepstakes entries, or even pharmacist forms are just waiting to be assembled with a high degree of accuracy—even if your customers don't approve or assist. Even a novice data assembler, identity hacker, can match home and business addresses to demographics and publicly available data and, like a video simulation game, begin playing out scenarios acting like hundreds to thousands of individual consumers.

Electronic data is everywhere and growing

In case you think the news media or a couple of individuals are overreacting to data theft and easy access to personal and confidential data, please go through this quick exercise.

Step 1. Go online to www.Google.com.

Step 2. Type "Attendee List" in search window.

Step 3. Select "Advanced Search," go to options under "File Type," and select "Microsoft Excel (.xls)"

Step 4. Click "Advanced Search" or hit "enter."

Step 5. Take a look at the Excel files presented. No, don't open them. They are private information.

Step 6. Edit the search box by adding "Mike" to the front of the search statement.

Step 7. Reexamine the files.

Hopefully, after a couple of people read this book, these files will become harder to access and will be more protected. Just maybe, companies, individuals, churches, and membership organizations will protect information more seriously.

Is this identity theft? This entire exercise takes about about 90 seconds, and if anyone has wised up to this application and no results appear, you can spend another 90 seconds experimenting with words like "name," "phone," "home," "addr_2," and other file types to see what pops up.

Get scared, exercise caution, and read your statements

You and your customers should be scared because customer data moves around much too easily. Customer data is easily monetized and too lazily shared.

A 16-gigabyte data storage card, the kind used in a camera, phone, or GPS, is the size of a thumbnail and weighs half an ounce. It can hold the name, address, phone number, email address, and information about every individual in the United States or the name and address of everyone in China. Sending that same amount of data as an email attachment takes less than 15 minutes on an easily available computer network.

Banking, health, credit card, and relationship data should not be directly traceable to individuals, families, households, and companies. Businesses and individuals exchange data too freely across unsecure networks, on pieces of paper, in mail, on the phone, in emails, and in web order forms.

This is an unfortunate artifact of antiquated systems design. As data is exchanged between companies, third parties, and outsourced service providers, the emphasis is on speed and efficient transaction processing. Individuals and customer data protection simply receives less attention.

Part of the issue is reliance on third parties for billing, collections, and customer service. Information needs to be portable and complete to reconstruct the customer situation. This is the only way to create situational awareness for all of the parties serving the customer and performing transactions and contacts on behalf of the company.

Information systems groups and technology companies have always had a blind spot when it comes to customer data management. This fundamental flaw comes from an incomplete vision, a short-sightedness in customer information design. The customer information is subservient to the demands of the transaction, accounting, and financial systems. This is why, to this day, it is so difficult to track all of the items in a customer order and all of the contacts preceding and following a customer transaction.

Businesses race to get new customers and minimize the customer's inconvenience, asking for substantial amounts of information in the process without even realizing it. As a result, customer information systems have been patched together, often based on tricking customers into believing that they are dealing with the same company or department. This is to promote the illusion that the customer has not been handed off to another department, another set of systems, or another company in another country. This deception has built an information network that is itself easily deceived.

Your business should use the CxC Matrix as a tool to audit your personal data protection policies and procedures at each contact point. The Matrix can list what business and personal data is exchanged and available at each contact point, what governance and safeguards exist at each point, whether data is encrypted or which data elements are exposed and why, where third party data usage agreements exist, and where data security and monitoring procedures are in place for each system.

Your business is challenged with reducing the amount of time that customers have to spend identifying themselves (authorizing transactions), while, at the same time, assuring the security and authenticity of each contact. In most instances, this identify requirement needs to take place prior to the exchange of any information in any contact. This all takes place before or simultaneously with preparing the contact point with the right message, the right offer, and all of the message components to ensure an optimum customer experience.

Businesses are failing the customer data protection test

First, there is no real test for ensuring that data is not misused, neglected, or shared unlawfully, intentionally or unintentionally. Customer data is just too portable.

There are a number of government and business groups taking this very seriously, but they are simply outgunned by opportunistic data pirates that game the system. Data pirates collect real dollars through fraud and extortion.

Government, regulatory, and trade organizations use a number of security, storage, encryption, and customer exchange standards, but Figure 11.1 shows that these are not working.

Note that a couple of the data breaches, particularly TJX and Heartland systems, were targeted by malicious computer software that stole data directly from the credit card processing servers and went undetected. While a single breach causes alarm and concern, the fact that these two highly reputable and specialized companies were breached and did not know it for extended periods of time is enough to justify paranoia.

Many of the companies listed on the table have gone through formal data and information systems audits to certify that they adhere to Sarbanes-Oxley (SOX), Graham Leach Bliley (GLBA), Payment Card Industry (PCI), or the Health Insurance and Portability and Accountability Act (HIPAA). Yet, these companies and many others like them are losing customer data at an alarming rate.

Most people will likely be shocked by the brands highlighted in the breached data table. How is it that our most trusted institutions in government, medicine, health care, financial services, and education lose so much data? They use names with addresses, Social Security numbers, and phone numbers. This data should never be together in a single database because doing so makes it an easy target for someone who wants to use it to apply for a loan, get a credit card, impersonate someone, or destroy someone's credit or reputation.

What are the odds that any of this information is yours? Likely.

Figure 11.1 below is a subset of one year's recent customer data breaches collected from publicly available sources. The list is frightening because of the millions of customers affected and the lack of adequate customer data protections.

Figure 11.1

Company		Alleged Number of Customers Exposed
TJX *2,400 stores,* *US & Europe*	Retail giant TJX said that a computer-security breach stretched back 10 months earlier than the company originally thought, compromising credit and debit card data, drivers' license numbers, and names and addresses.	45,700,000
Express *Scripts*	Express Scripts received an extortion letter including personal information on 75 members, including their Social Security numbers, addresses, dates of birth, and in some cases, prescription information." <div align="right">—Express Scripts website</div>	50 million prescriptions
Horizon *Blue Cross* *Blue Shield* *(Newark, NJ)*	More than 300,000 members' names, Social Security numbers, and other personal information were accessed on a stolen laptop computer.	300,000
Kraft Foods *(Northfield,* *IL)*	A stolen company-owned laptop contained names, maybe Social Security numbers of customers.	20,000
MTV *Networks* *(Los Angeles)*	Confidential employee data breached from outside: names, birth dates, Social Security numbers, compensation.	5000
HPY— *Heartland* *Payment* *Systems* *(Princeton,* *NJ)*	According to *The New York Times,* thieves stole data undetected from May 2008 to late fall 2008. More than 500 financial institutions were affected. Customers included more than 250,000 businesses ranging from restaurants to retailers to payroll systems.	Unknown total number of individual customers; 100 million credit card transactions monthly
Pennsylvania *Department* *of State* *(Harrisburg,* *PA)*	Voter website programming error allowed anyone on the Internet to view voter data: name, date of birth, driver's license number, political party. Some had last four digits of Social Security number.	30,000

For a running list of data breaches reported on a monthly basis, see
www.privacyrights.org/ar/ChronDataBreaches.htm

Protect your customers, protect your business: identification, authentication, and authorization

Business, accounting, and financial practices have not evolved to accommodate the needs of a digital age, which requires a whole different mindset regarding identification, authentication, and authorization. Each of these functions is required for every customer contact, but in the new digital world, each element has to be treated separately in order to ensure a customer's privacy. Companies that take short cuts in order to complete transactions and data exchanges more quickly and efficiently continue to be vulnerable to fraud.

Consumers have personas based on where they live, where they shop, what they buy, and how they buy. Your company needs to leverage this information, most of which you already have, in order to more rigorously identify customers and more closely meet your customers' expectations. This approach is not new and is most often used in fraud detection on credit card processing networks, but it is obviously not used enough or used correctly. This process works better for repeat customers than first time customers, but it should be reasonably executed by most companies.

According to a report by the Ponemon Institute, a Tucson-based research group, customer data breaches cost companies about $200 per customer with 40 percent of the cost attributed to losing customers to lack of trust and confidence. While breached data and identity theft are not the same issue, customers suffer the damages and pay the expense of repairing their information and reputation. Customers are the most vulnerable and least in control of their own information.

Customers should be paid when companies use their data

One solution to the customer data problem may be to require customers to manage their own data, which might also mean that only companies with customer permission can access customer data. In other words, no company would be allowed to use the data unless first approved by the customer.

Moving data control and access to the customer might also involve customers selling their own data to companies for marketing, research, and list sales as is already taking place today. But customers would receive a statement telling them who is using the data and they would be able to control the types of use. The conclusion is that customers should be rewarded for sharing their data and should also be provided a data usage statement showing which companies use and store data; for which transactions and purposes; where the data is used and stored; how often and recently the data was accessed; and the purpose.

Companies using customer-owned and managed data would have a lower fraud rate and a vested interest in ensuring that the customer information is absolutely verifiable. Customer-owned data would also relieve companies of any implied liability from misuse or incorrect data—two issues that are likely to grow in the coming years as more information is digitized and customer transparency broadens.

CHAPTER 12

Matrix Benefit and Use by Function and Department

In the 21st century, everyone in a company has a sales, marketing and service function, so every employee in every department needs to have the big marketing picture and know how he or she fits in. This chapter explains how the CxC Matrix can be used function-by-function, department-by-department to get the entire company focused on the customer.

The new marketing

The average U.S. consumer receives several million marketing messages a year, ranging from 3 million for relatively insular and disconnected customers to well over 100 million per year for heavy Internet users, mall shoppers, game players, and television and video watchers.

In a constant battle to get customer attention, marketers leverage every inch of text and electronic space and every second of customer face time. Marketing messages appear in every contact both intentionally and unintentionally.

Just as the number of messages sent to customers has exploded, the burden of responding to customers—including creating and managing customer contacts across every channel and consumer stage—has created unsustainable demands on marketing, customer support, advertising, and sales.

Customer contact management across departments

Many department resources support customer contact management across customer support, advertising, marketing, sales, and fulfillment. Resources are limited, and the demands of meeting every customer's needs seven days a week across any mix of circumstances and at every potential customer contact is unreasonable and unsustainable. You cannot afford to grow marketing staff, call center personnel, IT web page designers, and copywriters in parallel with message volume requirements.

There is no more time or tolerance for traditional marketing, advertising, sales, service, and IT infrastructures that communicate with customers disconnectedly and with tunnel vision that is concerned only with a limited view of selected contacts and channel niches.

Messages must be designed, delivered, measured, and refined in drastically compressed timeframes to meet customer expectations. Near-time communications, automated responses, and recommendations require faster and faster execution times. They must approach zero message delivery latency for web and electronic messages, i.e., automated electronic bidding; conditional, environmental, and rules-based product pricing; device self-diagnostics; and unattended upgrades.

Message design, execution, measurement, and refinement time compression

Figure 12.1

Channel	Time		What's Next?
	Then	Now	
Broadcast TV	6–9 months	1–12 weeks	YouTube, Cam2Web
Direct Mail	3–5 months	1–2 weeks	direct to print
Sales/Field Training	3–6 months	1–3 months	sfa/crm tools
Newspaper Print	2–4 weeks	1–2 weeks	digital press
Magazine	3–6 months	2–3 months	digital/v press

| Channel | Time | | What's Next? |
	Then	Now	
Brochure	1–4 months	1–3 weeks	direct to print
Signage	1–4 months	1–8 weeks	digital signs, web connected
Website	1–4 weeks	day parts	multi-party, dynamic content
Email	weekly	daily	triggers, dynamic content
Blogs, social networking	2–7 days	day parts	continuous, near time

Whereas technology and delivery mechanisms have changed, the core elements of direct marketing and direct communication have not. The CxC Matrix addresses each of the four key elements used for decades by direct marketers to govern message and contact design: List, Offer, Creative, and Media. The percentages represent each component's traditional contribution to a contact's performance.

List	50%	who and when	Targeting and segmentation
Offer	20%	what and why	What's the deal?
Creative	10%	copy and art	Interesting, entertaining, attention-getting
Media	20%	contact	Channel, sequence, frequency

Your company needs a playbook

The CxC Matrix defines the marketing and communications roles for managing customers across the entire customer life cycle for each corporate department and business function.

The CxC Matrix framework, combined with the CxC Matrix Treatment Map and message libraries comprise your company's playbook, which describes how the company will achieve its mission, strategy, and objectives executed in each contact and monitored through CxC Matrix reports.

Managing hundreds to thousands of dynamically changing contacts without a cohesive, corporate-wide structure and playbook dooms a company to:

- Overspend on under-performing contacts and issues,
- Under-fund highest return opportunities,
- Waste customer and company time and money repeating broken steps,
- Overpay for new business, excessive cost of sales, and
- Create highly inaccurate forecasting.

Now let's take a look at the specific ways your company might use and benefit from the CxC Matrix.

Executive Management

Strategy

The CxC Matrix deliberately aligns corporate objectives and goals with customer values and preferences depicting customer worthiness at every customer to company contact. Thus, it links department and individual decision results directly to customer performance. Linking strategy to activities provides clear direction to all stakeholders and provides a means for each employee to clearly delineate his or her role in overall customer success.

Visualizing and managing customer centricity

Many CEOs freely use the term "customer centricity" and tout the "customer-centric" aspects of their corporate initiatives and strategies. Quick research using Google and entering the terms "customer centric" and "annual report" returns over *29,000 references*. It lists the "customer-centric" claims and proclamations of thousands of companies. Yet most executives equate "customers" with sales and "customer performance" with "customer satisfaction" or

"Net Promoter Score," all of which are lagging performance measures. Worse yet, who at the company owns "customer" and "customer performance?" Two individuals? Two departments? All employees need to clearly see their role in the customer's context, how their decisions and job performance impact customer value.

Fixing the disconnect between strategy and activity

Despite talk about being customer-centric, rarely does executive and consulting rhetoric connect to execution or to employee activities, responsibilities and reward systems. As a result, few employees understand their connection to customers. They do not bother to learn how the decisions they make affect customers because, "that's not my job." Few employees can describe their company's end-to-end customer experience or the stages of their consumers' buying cycle.

The CxC Matrix depicts the roles of departments and managers as these roles relate to customers. Strategy is directly connected to goals, tactics, and actions with clear and simple ongoing performance measurements.

Transparency from decisions to effects

It is much easier for employees to get enthusiastic about customers than it is to generate enthusiasm for intangible metrics. The CxC Matrix helps company leaders rally employees around a common goal: customer value growth, while clearly delineating the customer contact points and responsible parties across the company.

The Matrix exposes the number of customers affected by a single decision and the resulting effects by customer, customer segment, market, and consumer cycle. Does offering a discount to a customer for his initial business result in greater customer lifetime value and loyalty, or do discounted customers always gravitate to the lowest cost provider? Do emails that remind customers about bill payments raise collections performance, or do phone calls to a select group of customer types perform better? And which customers have greater longevity? Measuring decision impact fosters accountability, collaboration, and innovation.

Although few employees can grasp their connection to financial performance numbers and the intricacies and mechanics of financial statements, using CxC Matrix visualizations, employees can see how their actions and decisions connect to customer behavior and performance, providing them with a sense of ownership and pride. Tying performance measurements directly to customer performance motivates employees to focus on specific activities that drive success.

The CxC Matrix lets executive managers see activities across the organization while measuring customer responsiveness and monetizing success.

Linking customer behavior to tactics supported by the company's strategy reduces learning cycle time, improving your company's nimbleness and visibility to market fluctuations, competitors, and unforeseen events.

The Matrix provides management tools for quickly assessing the cost and benefit opportunities of new initiatives, product offers, mergers, acquisitions, and market entries by linking the company's resources and processes to customer opportunities. The Matrix can be used to generate market and customer simulations across a multitude of scenarios to expose the resource, cost, revenue, risk, market, and customer impact.

Innovation and leadership

A manager's expanded view of internal operations and activities in the customer's context often uncovers numerous opportunities for repurposing, repackaging, and repricing services, while also uncovering untapped customer needs. Continuous observation of where, how, when, with whom and under what circumstances customers use and access your products and services often spawns innovation and new market discoveries.

Corporate guidance is executed at each customer contact and measured for its effectiveness on an ongoing basis to ensure that the company is operating in synchronization with customer needs to fully realize market potential.

Budget allocation

Executives use the Matrix to weigh the benefits of competing budget requests using impact-per-customer as the criteria for "go" and "no go" decisions.

Departments weighing investment decisions for new initiatives should be required to demonstrate the cost and revenue associated with their recommendations. The Matrix highlights which specific customers and segments will be affected and the associated revenue and cost consequences, while also quickly highlighting operational and time-to-market issues.

The Matrix provides an alert when multiple departments' decisions affect the same customers and a means to overlay multiple department and corporate initiatives to uncover potential tactical, process, departmental, and customer conflicts.

Executive Management CxC Matrix deliverables

- **Visualize:** Company-wide strategy by customer.

- **Analyze:** Weave customer metrics into corporate decision-making.

- **Monetize:** Resource investment measured by yield per customer.

- **Prioritize:** Target resources and investments at ROI initiatives.

- **Optimize:** Establish procedures, measurements, and reward systems to promote continuous performance improvement customer-by-customer and contact-by-contact.

Finance

Financial managers use the CxC Matrix in conjunction with other financial tools to assess enterprise-wide and departmental cost and revenue at a budget line and departmental level. The Matrix provides a means to assess, quantify, and monitor budget and resource decisions based on customer

impact and is especially useful to complement other risk and decision scenario assessment tools.

Accountability

The Matrix helps finance managers observe business performance by customer and by contact. This information is directly linked to the responsible
manager, systems, and activities, providing exceptional insight into revenue
and cost drivers. Contacts and activities tied directly to business owners and
measured by customer performance provide improved budget and resource
governance and monitoring. Financial analysts can assess the impact of cost
reductions or budget reallocations by the impact per customer, as well as
uncover unforeseen negative impacts.

For example, you can study cost reduction in a call center, changing hours
of operation for a particular office, or charging for a previously free service
and run through scenarios to project customer impact and the resulting
impact on revenue and costs.

Activity-based costing from a customer basis

If your company uses activity-based costing methods to scrutinize department and company budgets, you can benefit from linking customer transaction costs, department activity costs, and the Matrix's projections for future
activities. The customer dimension adds additional insights into "what if"
scenario planning, cost allocation, and cost attribution dynamics.

The Matrix is designed to connect and relate products, expenses, activities, lines of business, overhead, and resources in the way that a customer
uses them. It explicitly shows which customers and which customer groups
are affected by resource and service changes.

Customer performance benchmarking

Financial and business analysts use the Matrix for monitoring "business as
usual" and exception management analysis by observing aggregate cus-

tomer and activity counts by channel, department, and activity. A fluctuation in any performance indicator alerts analysts to an unforeseen and unanticipated change in business. Analysts are able to quickly isolate the abnormal area and drill down to the causes while alerting departments about downstream impact and changes to revenue and cost forecasts.

Explaining finance to internal clients using customers as a metric

Business analysts, statisticians, and people responsible for designing mathematical models and business simulations can use the Matrix visualization as a backdrop to explain how predictive models and root cause analysis is performed and where the results of their work can be put into action. The Matrix provides a means for modelers and business analysts to explain how decisions made in one contact or stage can affect performance. The Matrix's graphics, with numbers included to delineate customer path, depict the business process in a manner that enables technicians and business managers to collaborate on building, measuring, and refining optimum solutions.

Fewer financial surprises

By providing transparency down to a customer and activity level and visibility across all customer life stages, the Matrix reduces the likelihood of financial performance surprises.

Finance CxC Matrix deliverables

- **Visualize:** Revenue flow and costs across the enterprise linked to customers and activities.
- **Analyze:** Set benchmarks and be alert for deviations. Alert managers to changes and financial reporting impact.
- **Monetize:** Monitor the cost and potential revenue of each customer and each customer contact.

- **Prioritize:** Projects, budget decisions, critical business areas and risks based on impact.
- **Optimize:** Continuously monitor contacts for opportunistic investment and cost avoidance.

Information Technology and Systems Management

The mower story

The mower story from earlier in the book implies that the Acme Company is in lockstep with the customer's needs, interests, and ability to pay. As has been pointed out, this is not by chance but by a carefully thought-out execution of multiple contacts with scripted messages purposely designed to drive the customer to act. This process illustrates the benefits of capturing and leveraging customer information across each contact for use in future contacts and programs.

Figure 12.2

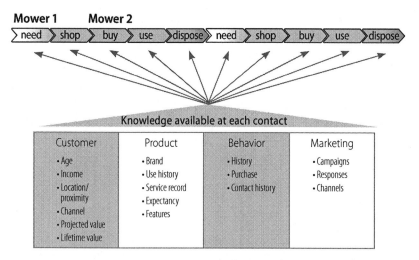

Maintaining a record of each customer's contacts, preferences, ability to pay, and particular nuances is no longer just inside the heads of the best performing sales people. Today, that information is contained in a variety of customer information files from internal and external sources.

This information ensures the best possible outcome at each customer contact point, from scope of offers to script messages. It can be used to alert downstream systems, schedule resources, and for inventory preparation—all in anticipation of the customer's next move. Information from each customer sequence can be recycled to benefit internal contact resources, partners, third parties, and even customers, as in the now famous Amazon web page message, "Customers like you also purchased . . . "

Structuring the mower program using the Matrix enabled each department to reuse the successful program elements without bearing significant expense and complexity for future programs. Additionally, isolating and documenting all of the program's elements enabled managers to test under-performing components while automating and reducing the cost of successful elements.

The Matrix does not assume a company has or will have to build a data warehouse in order to intelligently manage each customer contact. The Matrix design assumes that data sources will constantly evolve in the ways they collect, capture, and store customer and contact data. Therefore, it is not reasonable or cost justifiable to consolidate all customer and contact information in one place. Instead, the Matrix represents data and functions that may exist in third party systems, partners, and vendor systems. It relies on the framework, business, and data integration exchanges and rules to deliver a cohesive and singularly transparent customer experience.

The CxC Matrix system analysis

The challenge for today's technology and information professionals is to design and manage a corporate customer architecture that reaches out across the company and across the Internet to integrate and transform vast volumes of available data as quickly as possible into information assets that generate new insights and realize new business opportunities.

Such an undertaking is no small task. Today's enterprise systems extend beyond the walls of the corporate data center to include customers, suppliers, partners, and electronic marketplaces. These systems interact with databases, application servers, content management systems, data warehouses, workflow systems, search engines, message queues, web crawlers, mining and analysis packages, and other enterprise applications.

It is important to note that "systems" is used to describe electronic systems as well as non-electronic systems, such as putting an envelope in a box, physically moving around a store, and handwritten notes indicating inventory counts and product notations. The Matrix is meant to capture and map every customer contact—intentional, unintentional, scripted, unscripted, firsthand, secondhand, or even corporate and customer folklore.

Figure 12.3

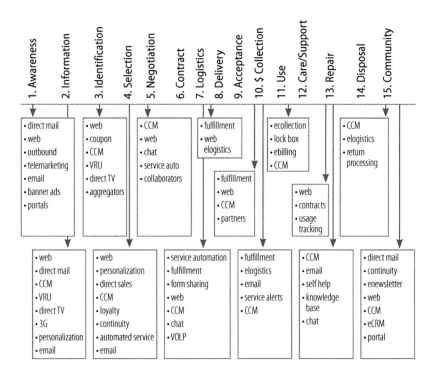

Technology investment decisions

Technology groups use the Matrix to weigh budget allocations for customer systems and customer system functionality as measured by the impact per customer or customer group. For example, a company seeking to purchase a customer relationship management system can demonstrate the value of the system by estimating the additional customer revenue that the system will generate by consumer and channel stage.

Additionally, when comparing proposed systems with similar functionality, the Matrix can be used to isolate the benefits of that functionality and its impact on the customer contacts.

Project management prioritization

Technology departments can use the Matrix to prioritize projects in a development queue and help allocate limited resources by plotting the areas that will be affected and the net benefit of each project, measured by increased customer revenue and decreased activity cost.

Figure 12.4 Sample List of CxC Matrix Systems

- Accounting
- Advertising
- Business intelligence
- Business performance management
- Business process management
- Call routing
- Care center inbound
- Compensation
- Contact management
- Content management
- Cost accounting
- Credit authorization
- Credit modeling
- CRM (customer relationship management)
- Customer service
- Customer survey
- Data matching
- Device design
- Device management
- Digital asset management
- Direct marketing
- Distribution
- Email hosting
- Email management
- Enterprise marketing management
- ERP (enterprise resource process) management
- Financial reporting
- Fraud detection
- Fulfillment
- Game management
- General ledger
- Inbound telemarketing
- Integrated communications
- Inventory
- IT operations
- Lead management
- Licensing
- List management
- Location security
- Logistics
- Maintenance
- Marketing automation
- Master data management
- Modeling
- Network design
- Offer management
- Order management
- Outbound telemarketing
- Packaging
- Partner management
- Performance management
- Performance reporting
- Point-of-sale
- Point-of-purchase
- Predictive modeling
- Printing
- Public relations
- Quality systems
- Resource management
- Returns processing
- Reverse logistics sales automation
- Security
- Self service
- Self service kiosk
- Self service mobile
- Self service phone
- Self service web
- Shipping
- Social media
- Statistics
- Subscription management
- Supply chain management
- Telephony
- Text-to-voice
- Voice-to-text
- Web analytics
- Web chat
- Web hosting
- Web presentation
- Web security
- Work flow

Visual aid for data and process mapping

Business analysts and information technology workers use CxC Matrix visualizations to scope database and data coordination designs across disparate systems, identifying integration points and data exchanges. The Matrix provides a schematic that connects customers to all company systems, including third party systems that are sometimes not considered part of IT planning.

The Matrix emphasizes and highlights the importance of process design from the customer's perspective, delineating success and failure points from a customer point of view while providing a performance metric for justifying process redesign or alternative resource investment.

Information Technology CxC Matrix deliverables

- **Visualize:** Comprehensive customer technology architecture; customer data movement; systems integration points; department to department connectivity; third party connectivity; process flow; customer information ecosystem; data, system, process gaps; world class customer infrastructure design.

- **Analyze:** Technology investments, prototype system designs, resource and technical alternatives, outsourcing, data quality, disaster recovery, security, system vulnerability, fraud.

- **Monetize:** Projects, IT investments, data, data quality, outsourced partners, expert systems.

- **Prioritize:** Resources, technology investments, solution areas, IT investment allocation.

- **Optimize:** Infrastructure, resource allocation, customer data process flows, reporting and alert systems, business process management initiatives.

Operations

Merchandising

The mower story might drive you crazy if you work in operations or if you own or manage a local store. You might think, "Am I supposed to have 20 lawn mowers of each variety stored at each location in the hope that someone might click on that email?"

In the background, the mechanics of this program started with a continuously running computer program, which detected that a particular store had too many lawn mowers in stock. The mower was then targeted for liquidation, and the company's analytical and operations technology linked together to propose scenarios designed to achieve the highest profit point by the fastest means possible.

The program calculated a number of liquidation options, including moving the mowers to another store, selling the mowers to a wholesaler, and returning them to the manufacturer. The inventory system noted that the mowers were assembled, which added costs and constrained liquidation options.

The program was designed to match company, finance, partner, and customer objectives respectively:

- Sell the product at the highest achievable margin,
- Gain new customers,
- Grow relationships, and
- Achieve optimum yield per customer.

The program evaluated the options for moving the lawn mowers through each of its channels, calculated the total costs, and predicted best customer and stakeholder outcomes. The program recommended that the mowers be promoted directly to the store's local market, to existing customers who lived within a 15-minute drive of the store, and who bought a similar or less-featured mower more than two years ago.

The program aligned the company's objectives with customer values and preferences to achieve the best outcome for the business and the customer.

The program performed these calculations and decision-making as a background process with no human intervention. The eventual program was put into motion from need to concept to initiation in less than three seconds.

Distribution

The Matrix delivers product demand and associated resource demand by channel, contact point, and time window, exposing most of the elements in the customer demand chain. Where possible, it connects the product or service needs and requests of specific customers to specific distribution outlets.

Advanced logistics, inventory management, and shipment planning systems can be linked to the Matrix to provide deeper insight into resource consumption, alternative delivery planning, and short-term, mid-term, seasonal, and long-term outsourcing opportunities.

Quality controls

The Matrix delineates the cost and revenue impact of poor quality products and service delivery by measuring it in lost revenue and increased customer management costs. These insights linked to the stages of the consumer cycle highlight where business processes or quality problems might jeopardize an entire product line, geography, line of business, or commercial channel such as ecommence.

Outsourcing

As outsourcing and co-sourcing continue to grow as resource solutions, you need to be able to measure their impact on customer flow, customer value and the entire consumer cycle. For example, do outsourced product repair services have a negative impact on repeat sales? Does one delivery process and set of vendors impact customer profitability differently than another alternative? Typically, these types of decisions are made with sparse data, gut instinct, and focus group surveys. However, the Matrix provides a means for experimenting with hypothetical scenarios and quantifying the customer impacts of changes. Then it provides a means for ongoing monitoring and measurement.

The customer perspective also provides the added benefit of parsing customer flows so that high value customers receive preferred treatment and resources while lower value customers are directed to lower cost solutions. Using the Matrix, you can experiment in share-gain relationships with outsourcers where the third party directly benefits in a proportional share of the increased yield per contact. Each contact should be evaluated as a platform for additional revenue streams, as well as an opportunity to grow the sponsor company's long-term customer value.

Vendor negotiations

You can use explicit customer flow metrics and their related revenues and costs to negotiate performance contracts with vendors and partners. Whereas some companies use customer survey samples or customer observation sampling at selected operational stages, the CxC Matrix provides a consistent operations metric covering all contacts (call backs, returns, complaints, unpaid items, etc.) overtime, pinning success to actual customer value.

Operations CxC Matrix deliverables

- **Visualize:** Product, service, and resource demand; supply chain linkages; demand chain; inability of vendor to coordinate with others; resource allocation; demand flow; inventory movement; customer management flow; world-class customer operations design.

- **Analyze:** Resource utilization, alternative resource configurations, just in time service/product opportunities.

- **Monetize:** Product and service outages, resource utilization, unused message slots, customer satisfaction, and vendor management.

- **Prioritize:** Process and system upgrades, critical path revenue and cost operations.

- **Optimize:** Supply chain, demand chain, vendor and supplier resources, distribution, asset management, facilities configuration, and expert contact management.

Human Resources

My company, my job from a customer's perspective

The CxC Matrix is the best tool for educating employees about how a business operates from a customer perspective. It lets employees walk the customer's path while showing the departments, managers, systems, and processes that support each consumer stage.

New employees, transitioning employees, and managers benefit from improved understanding of the functions related to meeting customer expectations. The performance numbers, customer value, customer lifetime revenue, and costs become clear and simple measures that employees grasp.

Employees also tend to feel a sense of responsibility when they understand the company's role in meeting customers' needs.

Education roles and goals

The Matrix provides employees with a sense of ownership, accountability, and responsibility, and human resources managers benefit from the employees' broader knowledge of corporate operations. This makes it possible to improve business problem-solving while stressing the importance of communication skills, reporting, quality efforts, and documentation.

The Matrix's trans-departmental and trans-functional design broadens employees' perspective regarding their individual impact on overall business. It makes them aware of the operations and provides some education regarding other departments, functions, and systems across the company.

The customer-eye view encourages employees to participate in suggesting solutions and making recommendations about improving operations, functions, and policies. Employees may uncover marketing, analytical, process design, or selling skill sets that would otherwise go unnoticed. The enterprise view assists in career development by providing employees with exposure to the skills required and the functions performed in other parts of the company.

Resource planning and scheduling

Managers and employees use the Matrix to observe customer flow and activity at different times of the day, different days of the week, and different seasons to appropriately schedule resources and ensure that the right skills are available at each critical customer contact point.

Pay performance and incentive design

Managers also use the Matrix and associated key performance indicators to evaluate employee job performance. The CxC Matrix creates simple, visible, and common benchmarks for monitoring ongoing job performance, as well as quantifying performance related to each employee's activities and decisions.

The CxC Matrix measures the value of individual employee decisions and activities on business growth and cost containment. Managers find the Matrix suitable for designing, monitoring, and executing incentive pay structures and performance rewards systems based on customer performance. The metrics are standardized in the system, providing consistency over time. Yet its breadth shows where upstream and downstream events and circumstances may positively or negatively influence performance.

Human Resources CxC Matrix deliverables

- **Visualize:** The customer journey across departments, functions, systems, and the employee's individual role.

- **Analyze:** Employee performance, interdepartmental processes, resource allocation, scheduling, payment, and reward systems.

- **Monetize:** The impacts of decision-making, activity, quality initiatives, and customer satisfaction.

- **Prioritize:** Specific functions within roles, department resource requirements.

- **Optimize:** Customer yield per employee.

Sales

A primary Matrix business objective is to make the company and the customer-facing resource in each contact look great, wise, helpful, and knowledgeable. The accumulation of previous contact success, customer information, marketing knowledge and successful resolutions learned and stored from similar customers allows the company to effortlessly deliver a perfect, profitable contact experience.

Salespeople (which includes everyone, since everyone is in sales) must understand:

- Where the customer is in the buying process,

- The channels and activities the customer conducted, and

- An estimate of the customer's next actions, timing, needs and contacts.

All of this must be balanced with the customer's potential value and the probability of achieving that value.

In a perfect system, the CxC Matrix not only shows what customers have done, but it predicts what they are likely to do next and when. The system alerts the salesperson and resources around the company when a customer does not act, and it provides them with the means to re-engage the customer through the right channel with the right message, offer, or recommendation. Then it monitors the potential outcome. It is important to remember that "do nothing" is often an option when a customer has a low probability of acting over the next 60 days and when the customer has a low probability of ever buying or making a customer referral.

You're invited to the 1% Success Party

Marketers and salespeople like to tell customer success stories like the one about the mower, emphasizing the excellent coordination, foresight, customer insight, analytics, and programming. But they shy away from discussing the fact that marketing and sales efforts rarely achieve double-digit success.

Less than one percent of most promotional email programs, direct mail, telemarketing, and other advertising programs result in a sale. The best salespeople achieve success rates of less than 10 percent per customer contact, and most of them achieve less than 1 percent.

Marketing does not put up banners that say, "We hit 1%!" Salespeople don't celebrate making 40 sales pitches to get a single meeting or to get one person to actually buy "the mower." The real opportunity in marketing and sales lies in the 99 percent of the wasted contacts.

One fallacy of traditional sales and marketing measurements was illustrated in the simple need, shop, buy example earlier in the book. Companies under-represent the number of contacts responsible for making the eventual sale or solving a customer problem. Yet all of the other contacts that the company conducts and funds likely contribute to the eventual sale. Companies that fail to recognize the contribution and value of all related contacts are in danger of under-investing or eliminating the contact points that ultimately persuade a customer to purchase.

The Matrix unveils the 99 percent of unmentioned contacts, plus all of the post-sale contacts, to expose hundreds of additional cross-sell, up-sell, referral, and affiliate revenue opportunities.

Examining the program from the business side demonstrates typical marketing and sales efficacy, while emphasizing the extreme importance of success at each consumer cycle. As fewer customers progress through the customer cycle, revenue success depends on fewer prospects, but more contacts.

In a multi-wave marketing program customers are targeted more than once and often across multiple channels in a predefined sequence using a set of rules to orchestrate follow-up contacts.

The mower program insights

The mower marketing program was one component in a multi-wave-marketing program. It matched multiple customer groups to multiple marketing, sales, and customer service programs.

Sales CxC Matrix deliverables

- **Visualize:** Customer pipeline by stage and channel activity; upcoming customer activities and stalled customers; revenue opportunities across the entire company; costly low potential prospects.

- **Analyze:** Return on sales channel, sales territories and rationale, opportunity potential versus sales resource constraints, seasonality, demand chain; pipeline barriers, downstream impact to customer lifetime value.

- **Monetize:** Customers, activities, sales investment, sales cycle, return per activity per channel, sales partners, markets, regions, revenue/lead cost per source.

- **Prioritize:** Activities and resource allocation, margin per product and service combinations, lead sources, existing relationships, portfolio management, partners.

- **Optimize:** Activities and resource allocation, lead generation and cost per lead by stage and channel, referrals, cross-sales, up-sells, affiliate sales, margin per sale, margin per customer.

Legal

Your company is vulnerable to liability at each stage of the CxC Matrix. From customer data breaches to misrepresentation of services, account mismanagement, negligence, physical injury, etc., the Matrix graphically represents every customer contact along with every company promise and obligation across all stages of the consumer cycle. Additionally, the Matrix provides managers with performance visibility and risk assessment capabilities that show responsibilities related to governance, performance reporting, performance disclosures, and material events.

The Matrix provides an overview of most of the customer liability areas, and it also provides a means for recovery, customer notification, and customer path re-creation that can be used to remedy the effects of an event, product, or service. The Matrix provides a means to quantify an event's exposure, the number of potential customers affected, and the contact points related to any incident.

The CxC Matrix can also be used to retrace a customer's communications, notices, and instructions, as well as all of his contacts—actual and assumed (based on probability of like customers). This allows you to comprehensively recreate a customer's entire relationship with your company. Consumer cycle re-creation provides you with a road map for where, when, and how often to provide customer instructions, warnings, support, and assistance regarding the uses and alternative uses of products.

Legal departments and corporate counsel should use the CxC Matrix to help customers manage their own relationships by providing a customer-centric road map that highlights all company, industry, market, legal, government, and trade sources. These references and guidance materials across each CxC Matrix stage serve as a virtual "You are here" map for every customer across the information gathering, purchasing, use, and disposal consumer cycles.

Legal departments should also consider geographic laws and regulations relative to product and service delivery. Countries, states, regions, towns, and channels have different governing bodies, each of which may require their own version of product and service delivery, disclosures, notifications, fees, and taxes. The CxC Matrix can be modified for each region to document and ensure compliance while providing material proof of your company's acknowledgement and enforcement. Likewise, you can analyze the impact, cost, and resources required when entering new markets and when regulation changes are being considered.

Note: Managers who move from one region to another should be briefed using the Matrix in order to highlight important customer notification, disclosure, liability, information, and treatment differences from their prior posts.

Issues of privacy

As customer treatments become more complex, dynamic, and multi-party, it is inevitable that legal and regulatory bodies will demand that companies provide greater transparency to the elements used for each treatment. With digitization and the speed of information exchanged between companies and from system to system, customers will demand to see how their personal information is used to determine pricing, customer service, or warranty coverage. Regulators will slowly seek to understand the mechanics of proprietary and dynamic pricing and offer systems, as well as their affect on fair trade, product distribution, and service distribution.

Likewise, customers will be within their assumed rights to ask companies to recreate the context and rules used to construct special offers, messages, and pricing.

Our data went where?

Data breeches will continue to grow as more information and transactions are digitized. As a result, personal and confidential information provided by customers will be continually at risk. Additionally, company information stores and data networks will continue to be pirated, poached, and hijacked, requiring companies to insist on additional third party customer authenticity validation and authorization among payment systems and partners.

Customer backlash is a likely result of the increased exposure of confidential data. Legal or governmental representatives may demand specific disclosures regarding how, why, when, where, and for what purpose customer information was stored, accessed, and modeled by companies other than the business customers believed they were dealing with directly. Transparency is ripe for continued scrutiny, whether to data vendors, credit bureaus, transaction processors, data exchange, integration companies, subsidiaries, or lines of business.

It is likely that companies will face not only growing legal and financial liability for misuse, mishandling, and negligence related to customer data, but also for not using customer data when that information could benefit the customer, as in the "Mad Cow" case reported in the *Washington Post* (July 6, 2004). Although some customers are troubled by the privacy implications of data capture, many assume that their information will be used to their benefit. Customers are likely to also assume that they should have access to their personal information in the company's context. They will want to see who had access to their information and how their information was used to conduct business. If these assumptions are not met, a negative customer experience could result.

In the "Mad Cow" case mentioned above, a female customer had purchased ground beef from a local market, using her customer loyalty card, which recorded every item she bought.

She used the beef to cook a holiday dinner and only a couple of weeks later learned from a newspaper article that 10,000 pounds of beef potentially tainted by mad-cow disease (MCD) had been recalled from stores in Western states, including hers. She read about another customer whose purchase had been recalled after he demanded that the store check his customer loyalty card to determine if the meat he had purchased was part of the recall.

The female customer then asked that her card be checked to verify the safety of the meat she fed to her family. However, the store made her make the request in writing and come to the store's office for the records. She eventually learned that the meat she had fed her family was part of the recall. The result was a lawsuit against the store, claiming that it had the ability to alert her to the recall and did not do so.

Legal CxC Matrix deliverables

- **Visualize:** Customer contacts and implied liability by life stage, channel, product, market, and region

- **Analyze:** Exposure, remedy scenarios, risk insurance coverage, partner/vendor liability

- **Monetize:** Cost to notify affected customers, scope of various legal scenarios, cost of compliance and governance, exposure and risk related to data handling

- **Prioritize:** Communications points, highest risk business areas, documentation, communication guidelines and procedures.

- **Optimize:** Issue discovery and escalation, insurance protection, risk prevention

Customer Service

"Eighty percent of 2,049 US adults surveyed decided never to go back to a business/organization after a bad customer service experience. The study clearly indicates that an organization's customer service level is a defining factor that will make or break a company."

— "Studies Reveal Consumer Reaction to Bad Customer Service", TMCNET.com

Companies invest millions of dollars in customer service and satisfaction surveys, brand research, awareness studies, and measures like Net Promotion Score and J.D. Power. Unfortunately, these same companies often find it difficult to persuade executives, workers, and shareholders that the information reported has a direct impact on company performance.

The Matrix measures how customers "vote with their feet" and does not rely on self-reported information or sample surveys from customers. However, traditional surveys and research techniques can greatly enhance the Matrix by isolating customers at individual stages and channels to poll them as to why they did or didn't move forward with a purchase decision, as well as why they purchased again. The Matrix can be used to identify pockets of customers who hold substantial potential revenue, cost, or risk. These groups of customers can be isolated, analyzed, polled, scrutinized, and tested to develop actionable, measurable business performance improvement initiatives.

The Matrix acts as a sensor across all customer contacts to alert each contact point regarding anticipated customer contacts, contact timing, volumes, and interests. The Matrix can also be used to capture best performing tactics and methods for quick replication across the rest of the customer contact points.

Since the Matrix tags customers at each stage in their process, your managers can anticipate contact flow when an increase in similar customer problems arise or when new marketing messages and promotions hit the market, resulting in increased volumes of customer phone calls, emails, and site visits.

The Matrix records customer service contacts and post-contact customer activities, providing the most reliable measure of problem resolution and customer satisfaction.

Eighty-nine percent of people who owned cars from a certain manufacturer said they were very satisfied, and 67 percent said they intended to purchase another car from that manufacturer. Fewer than 20 percent actually did.

In another survey, nearly half of consumers said poor service led them to change service providers in at least one industry in the past year. When asked to further explain their reasons for switching, the greatest number of these respondents (61 percent) identified poor service or product quality; to get lower prices (46 percent); a service representative's lack of knowledge about a provider's services or products (39 percent); lack of customized solutions (22 percent); company policies that create bureaucracy (19 percent); and technologies that delay or stop service (19 percent).

"Poor Customer Service is Top Reason Consumers Switch Service Providers, Accenture Survey Finds," *Business Wire*, 7/26/05

Root cause problem analysis

Customer problems don't start in customer service; they end up there. The CxC Matrix tracks customers from awareness through disposal. Customer service representatives and customer process designers can trace problems back to their root cause because the Matrix tracks every company, product, partner, and community contact. It replays the whole story from the customer's perspective.

Customer Rage Points across the CxC Matrix

The *2005 National Customer Rage Study*, sponsored by the *Customer Care Alliance* (CCA) in collaboration with the W.P. Carey School of Business at the University of Arizona, provides insight into the causes and consequences of customer rage. The study focused on the most serious problems experienced by individuals (random sample of U.S. households) with products and services during the period August 2004 through August 2005.

Seventy percent of all respondents reported rage with customer service due to (in order of occurrence):

1. Unsatisfactory product (includes financial products);
2. Unsatisfactory service;
3. Incorrect/deceptive billing;
4. Unsatisfactory repair;
5. Product/service is not as agreed upon;
6. Deceptive advertising/packaging/pricing; and
7. Dealer/salesperson misrepresented the product/service.

The most common "damages suffered" included loss of time (53%); loss of money (30%); and physical injury (5%).

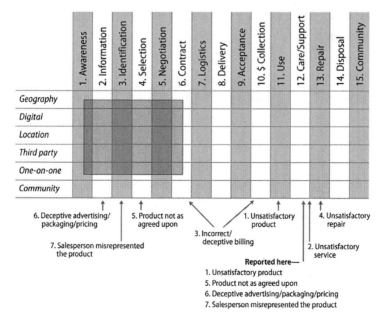

Mismanaged contacts spawn additional costs across a company in obvious areas like shipping, repair, call handling, and returns, but the Matrix also quantifies additional costs caused by forfeited future business, negative word-of-mouth, and customer replacement. The Matrix clearly shows the cost of mismanaged contacts with a high potential-value customer and market segment. But it also provides a comprehensive view of the resources and options for rectifying or rerouting high potential–value customers through alternative process and customer paths.

Help yourself

The Matrix is designed to help you design self-service processes and guidelines so that customers can self-navigate their own solutions or contribute to building better solutions.

Managers use the Matrix to plot customer service recovery and care contact procedures, paths, best practices, and metrics. The Matrix provides a unique view of problem resolution that exposes alternative channels and resources along with a customer-specific historical view of all steps and channels that a customer has journeyed.

As technology becomes more advanced, you may be embedding service recovery tools, alerts, and notifications in your products. One obvious example is a car service alert that notifies a customer that service is recommended in 1,000 miles. Another example is a printer notification message that alerts service companies and suppliers. Still another is a new product reminder delivered to a sales prospect based on prior inquiries, which uses the estimated life expectancy and replacement cycle of the selected product. It may also include a special financing offer for the new product.

You should perform a similar exercise for your business to chart customer paths and highlight where customer recommendations should be inserted. These will add value to a customer's overall experience and generate contacts to ensure future business and revenue, both direct and indirect.

Improved customer management—using Situational Awareness

Situational Awareness (SA) is one of the CxC Matrix's fundamental design principles. In customer service, Situational Awareness can be defined as understanding what is happening with the customer so you can figure out how to help.

The CxC Matrix uses situational awareness principles to prepare customer-facing personnel for assessing customer situations and solutions. More importantly, SA is used as a basis for automating the many decision functions required to support unattended situations where an employee is not engaged in a company decision.

Generating revenue from captive contacts

You can use a sophisticated telephone system that intelligently routes calls based on caller ID, customer registration, or neighborhood information. This determines which call center, customer service representatives (CSRs), treatment, and offer the caller will receive. The telephone system exchanges data with the offer management system, order management system, and customer management systems to continuously monitor and reprioritize call and offer allocations. This refines the allocations based on offer performance, resource availability, and contact success. The intelligent call routing system usually reduces call center costs because calls from both new and repeat customers are resolved quickly and to everyone's satisfaction.

Outsourcing agreements and business processes

Your company can continue to seek opportunities to outsource customer contact functions, customer support, email hosting, offer design and management, copywriting, and product and service design and automation. You should knowingly choose which contacts you must maintain in-house or under direct management in order to leverage your company's core competencies. Then you must monitor the strategic fitness and cost benefit of outsourcing every other function. The Matrix provides a means for you to dictate explicit service levels and process level terms for any outsourcing arrangement, while also providing performance visibility measured by customer.

Customer Service "Think Like a Customer" deliverables

- **Visualize:** Individual customer paths, aggregate customer paths, detailed customer interaction directory, best-in-class contact design.

- **Analyze:** Customer service resource allocation, root cause problem analysis, contact flow, resolution processes, partner and affiliate contacts, customer satisfaction relative to customer paths.

- **Monetize:** Value per customer, contact, call incident, resolution, revenue saved per customer, add-on revenue per customer, customer cross-sells, up-sells, and referrals.

- **Prioritize:** Match resources to opportunities, isolate problem sources, high potential customers, low performing contact points.

- **Optimize:** Resolution path, customer referral process, customer review process, customer successes, and best practice process templates.

Customer Relationship Management—CRM

The true measure of CRM is change that impacts each customer in each contact. Customers expect simplicity.

Many companies have invested billions of dollars on Customer Relationship Management (CRM) systems, implementations, consulting, and outsourcing. Yet customer satisfaction scores continue to decline, and customer rage and frustration continues to grow.

How can it be that these enormous investments have created less satisfied and more disgruntled customers?

Figure 12.5

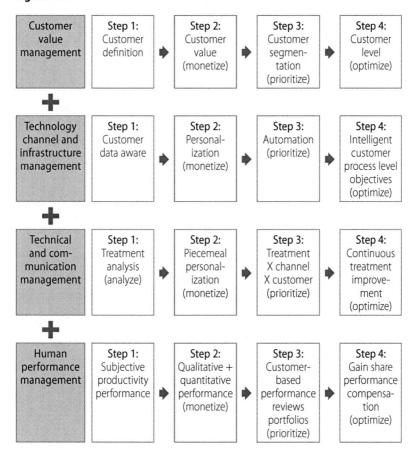

The CRM label includes everything from call center systems to predictive modeling and data marts. The smartest firms and consultants have pieced together solutions, frameworks, and methodologies. They have written books and guides, and they have conducted endless sessions on best practices and proven methods. Still, customers are dissatisfied.

Of course, the breadth of what is classified and sold as CRM is part of the problem. CRM is just too unwieldy. But the biggest issue has to do with projects that are initiated with little regard for how a customer's experience will change after the investment. What will be different the next time the customer makes a phone call? What will be different when the customer visits a store or website, opens an envelope, or uses the product or service? The result of the customer's changed contact should be the single, clear objective of each CRM investment. Will the contact generate more revenue? Will it cost less but achieve the same level of revenue, or neither? Figure 12.5 illustrates CRM maturity stages that apply to both business-to-consumer companies and business-to-business companies across most industries.

Use the CxC Matrix to visualize CRM

Most business managers and executives are overly polite when it comes to discussing CRM. It sounds foolish to say out loud, "We are not concerned with customer management." Once, when working with a major telecommunications firm, I was asked to meet with a group of the company's regional presidents and their CRM team. The company had spent nearly $150 million on CRM technology and a multiple of its technology investment on implementation and training over the prior two years. I was invited to discuss "CRM Strategy" and to help them answer, "What went wrong and how to fix it." After introductions, we started the meeting with a simple question directed to each of seven presidents, "What did you expect would be different after CRM's successful launch?"

While each answer was slightly different, they all circled around cost reduction, improved customer satisfaction, improved customer performance visibility, and faster/less expensive problem resolution. The information and technology participants and the external consultants responsible for the project had slightly different answers. However, neither group answered based on what the customer would experience differently the day after the successful launch.

You can't manage what you can't see

To get everyone to agree on a definition of CRM, I sketched out a rough 15 X 6 CxC Matrix drawing on the large whiteboard. I quickly explained that each cell represented a customer contact point across the buying stage and each row represented a channel category. Then came the big question. "Which cells did you expect to impact with your CRM initiative?"

This was the most uncomfortable part of the meeting by far. The head of information technology came to the front of the room and put X's in boxes under "care and support, repair, collection and delivery" and declared, "That is what was in scope."

The rest of the group sat quietly and stared at the empty space in the remaining 83 cells.

"The purpose of a company is to create a customer . . . The only profit center is the customer . . . Therefore the business has two—and only two—basic functions: marketing and innovation. Marketing and innovation produce results: all the rest are costs."

—Peter F. Drucker

CRM "Think Like a Customer" deliverables

- **Visualize:** Total customer experience, customer performance by department, customer handling and communication procedures.

- **Analyze:** Resource allocation, customer flow and routing alternatives, resource capabilities match to market needs by contact, contact resource fitness.

- **Monetize:** Customer activity cost, resource costs, customer potential, opportunity costs.

- **Prioritize:** At-risk customers, customer defection points, underused contacts, customer bottlenecks, customer growth areas, resources, alternative sources.

- **Optimize:** Customer value, internal customer communication processes.

Marketing Feeds Matrix Slots Contact by Contact

The CxC Treatment Map

The CxC Treatment Map exposes the most granular level of the CxC Matrix: the messages and rules executed at each slot in each customer contact. Filling the slots is most often the responsibility of your marketing department. Your marketing department likely manages advertising messages through an agency, sales, corporate relations, vendor relations and service messages through those respective departments all of which are coordinated and choreographed to sustain the company's brand value and profit margin.

The Treatment Map evaluates how well each contact meets your corporate objectives. It can identify opportunities for improvements and can uncover misalignments between customer needs, business objectives and actual treatments.

The Treatment Map verbally walks through the current and potential treatments and encourages participation from all of the related departments and third parties. Again, each scenario and component is monetized using actual or estimated values in order to test and build the best performing customer experience solutions.

Companies using marketing automation systems, marketing resource management, campaign management, offer management and advanced contact management systems likely have the essential tools and know how to extend these systems capabilities to the broader task of managing slots and treatments across the entire breadth of the CxC Matrix. The Treatment Map fosters collaboration across multiple departments and disciplines to create an unparalleled transparency to the customer experience for all of the parties responsible for creating, hosting, transacting, measuring, and modeling each contact and contact stream.

Treatment Map Example

The CxC Matrix Treatment Map sample excerpt that follows depicts the company's current treatments and contact delivery systems, channels, managers, objectives, and system capabilities. Each cell in the Matrix Treatment

Map has a corresponding monetization formula that tracks the cost and potential revenue projected for each treatment and treatment combination.

Figure 12.6

Channel/ medium	Response channel	Systems	Personalization?	Disposition	Current treatment	Current segmentation
Direct mail Print Email Web ads	Internet	website	yes, using script and dept. designed rules	place order	configure order, accept	customer offer by channel
DR-TV				abandon order	volume dependent	customer offer by channel
				do-not-contact request	add to DNC list	customer offer by channel
Direct mail Web ads Print	phone	agent web-based order entry	yes, using script and dept. designed rules	do-not-contact request	add to DNC list	customer offer by channel
Direct mail Print DR-TV	mail	order management	none (batch input)	do-not-contact request	add to DNC list	customer offer by channel
DR-TV	phone agent	order management	none (batch input)	do-not-contact request	add to DNC list	customer offer by channel

Potential segmentation	Segment	Objective	Immediate treatments	Follow-up treatments
Offer code, order info, product, survey, real-time enhancement, "likely-to-buy-x zip code" model, Predictive Model set, credit card authorization, customer history, pay method, do-not-call	high attrition risk	retain, reduce cost	credit card, reject order, alternate offer	
	low attrition risk	up-sell, loyalty	up-sell offer, survey, MGM, sample	
	credit auth reject	sell	request other card or check	exclusion list?
	back order	retain	offer alternative, notify	notify, offer alternative, offer consolation gift
(same as above)	refusals	sell	send info, alternate offer, catalog, sample	new offer, catalog, third-party offer, newsletter, event notices
offer code, geography, real time calculation	high potential	sell	find contact preference	new offer?
	low potential	reduce cost	exclusion list	
(same as above)	(same as above)	(same as above)	none (batch process)	outbound contacts
(same as above)	(same as above)	(same as above)	meet objections, accept order, send literature	outbound contacts

CxC Matrix Treatment Map Deliverables

- **Visualize:** Advertising, Brand exposures, advertising campaigns, interdepartmental customer messaging

- **Analyze:** Channel spend allocation, competitor messaging and channel execution, treatment execution turnaround time, execution and measurement systems, internal versus third party capabilities, creative vs. offer vs. list vs. channel, cost benefit of continuous treatment optimization

- **Monetize:** media spend, channel spend, brand impact, communication design, agency tactics, margin lift, contact technology enhancements, market segments.

- **Prioritize:** Media, contact points, message combinations

- **Optimize:** Media spend, agency spend, offer execution, campaigns, sales, service and marketing initiatives

Marketing Performance Measurement

In an era when marketers are increasingly asked to prove the value of their efforts, those who lack a complete view of all customer contacts cannot be sure that they have considered all possibilities when deciding on marketing strategy. They cannot accurately compare the costs and benefits of different opportunities to be sure they are spending money effectively. The CxC Matrix gives them this view.

Matrix data is purposely designed for automation, predictive analysis, and business simulation. It creates a means and structure for continuous performance improvement and provides a framework for observation and experimentation.

Digitized data generated by customer transactions and interactions, combined with product and service use information, can be used to dramatically alter business decisions. Given enough parameters, systems can estimate what an individual customer can do and factor that assessment against what similar customers in similar situations did. This makes customer behavior more predictable and actionable. More importantly, it creates an analytical construct that accelerates company learning and reduces discovery time. Capturing this complexity requires a disciplined mapping process. The CxC Matrix starts with the set of contact points available to your company based on how it advertises, sells, delivers, and services its products. Although large, this data set is finite.

Automate what works—Continuous and Automatic Selling

With multiple sales, service, and communications programs running, customers responding through multiple channels (phone, in-store, and website), and customers at various stages of purchase, there is too much information for any person or department to manage. By the time a marketing manager examines the results of any aspect of the program in detail, tens of other programs have been launched, and thousands of contacts have been spawned across multiple channels.

Figure 12.7 Relative Need for Automated Rules

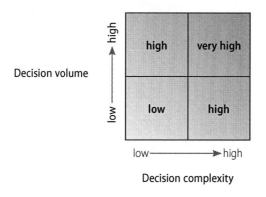

Continuous and Automatic Selling (CAS), applies proven direct marketing testing and analysis principles to each individual customer contact. It does this by using business rules to determine the elements served to each slot, container and slot, and container combinations.

At its simplest, the CAS constantly tests the current elements versus potential alternative elements until the challenger out-performs the base, "Offer A," in the example below.

When the "challenger" out-performs the base, the challenger replaces the base, and a new challenger from the "Test" or pending challenger set replaces the "Challenger."

This practice, while not commonplace, is used extensively on websites that dynamically present offers and content based on a visitor's (customer's) profile data (if registered), website navigation path, click stream, geographic location, and any other accessible data.

Companies are using similar methods to dynamically construct emails to customers who identify their preferences and Matrix consumer stage to assemble each email's contents: messages, offers, colors, graphics, follow-up channels, pricing, contact instructions, and partner offers.

Figure 12.8 Continuous Contact Optimization

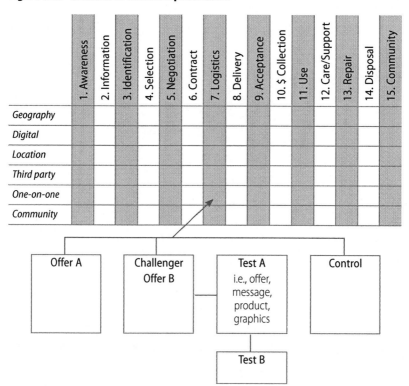

Figure 12.9 Making Contacts Manageable and Observable

	1. Awareness	2. Information	3. Identification	4. Selection	5. Negotiation	6. Contract	7. Logistics	8. Delivery	9. Acceptance	10. $ Collection	11. Use	12. Care/Support	13. Repair	14. Disposal	15. Community
Geography															
Digital															
Location															
Third party															
One-on-one															
Community															

While early adopters and technically sophisticated companies may seek to quickly optimize every possible contact in each channel at each Matrix stage, this is a very expensive and complex proposition. It is also not likely to be necessary to achieve the majority of the revenue and profits available through optimizing performance in a few strategically selected channels. It is also worth noting that, as evidenced in the following example, additional capital generates higher returns when directed at increasing the frequency and complexity of current offers, products, and messages. This requires more people and more creative service and product offerings. It generates more to talk about and more people to create stories.

Best story wins!

A highly successful company that had experienced a 20 percent annual growth rate for a number of years—primarily due to leveraging web and Internet channels in combination with their traditional channels—found that it needed to expand its staff of copywriters from two or three people per line of business to 20 or 30 per line of business. This was the only way that it could meet the demands of constantly constructing new offers, new messages, and various pricing and marketing techniques.

Did it pay off? Yes. Growth expanded to over 30 percent year over year in a highly competitive market, and some individual lines of business grew profits in excess of 50 percent. Profits grew due to the reduced cycle time in identifying winning programs and reducing the wasted expense of under-performing and failed programs that atrophied in the market.

The high-profit, high-growth company's CEO, who has an account-ing background, made substantial investments in performance manage-ment systems technology. He empowered his chief technology officer and chief operations officer to invest in systems and processes that provided quick, efficient, and flexible execution of dynamically changing offers and products.

His ultimate success came from their managers with a set of metrics and reports available in near real time and showed the value of nearly every element of each contact. Every manager was encouraged to monitor yield per offer, yield per customer, lifetime customer value, and yield per contact, including cross-sales, up-sells, and referrals. Sales by customer were also monitored but, more importantly, were valued for their internal cross-sell potential.

His mantra was, "Best Story Wins," and he set up a customer infrastruc-ture capable of identifying, which stories were best performing. He provided managers with the tools to continuously manufacture, monitor, test, and execute the "best stories," sales propositions, and customer experiences in their chosen markets.

Marketing Performance CxC Matrix deliverables

- **Visualize:** Brand impressions, competitors messaging strategy; messaging flow for new versus existing customers' marketing; sales, communications strategies; geographic/competitor specific messaging strategy; communications plan; product lifecycle; consumer lifecycle; innovation vulnerability; style book.

- **Analyze:** Potential customer revenue by life stage; customer profitability ranges per contact combinations; customer value performance algorithm; market simulation; promotion simulation; market disruption simulation; merger and acquisitions, new market entry; product launch; product/service discontinuation; management hypothetical simulations; war room analysis.

- **Monetize:** Customer data elements, process and resource attributes, mergers and acquisitions, new market potential, price change impact, service alternatives, market components, competitors and partners pricing, distribution, and profitability.

- **Prioritize:** Performance outliers that indicate high business risk and untapped revenue potential; keystone consumer cycle events and tactics; markets, products, customers.

- **Optimize:** Customer potential algorithm performance; slot and contact component combinations; market observation data and criteria; decisioning cycle time support; and tools for all management.

How you can use the CxC Matrix today

Your company's version of the CxC Matrix, channels by customer stage, should be clear in every decision-maker's mind and readily available at every manager's disposal to depict how any business decision will affect customers and potential upstream and downstream corporate impacts. How and where does this decision impact customers? How many customers of which segments will be affected? Which channels are best suited to introduce an offer, change, or announcement to customers?

The CxC Matrix is meant to depict the obvious but often overlooked channels and vehicles for conveying messages to customers. The same Matrix that was used at the planning stage can be used post decision to assess the accuracy of the assumptions made at the time of the decision.

A simple Matrix should become part of managers' project proposals to delineate the anticipated impact on customers by life stage and contact point. Will the proposed project grow customer flow? Reduce customer flow to specific contact points? Grow or reduce revenue and costs at specific contact points?

Ongoing Matrix uses

Most companies have reporting capabilities whereby they can create standard management reports using the CxC Matrix design and principles, reporting on customer flow and customer value across departments and systems on a quarterly, monthly, daily, or near term basis.

The Matrix is designed to provide an enterprise view of customer performance and as such is often fed data from a number of disparate internal and external systems. The company's requirements for level of Matrix detail and the frequency of reporting dictates the amount of design and programming resource required. Department and function specific CxC Matrix reporting and systems can be designed and launched using internal resources or a combination of external resources, hosted reporting services, and any number of hybrid resource configurations.

Advanced CxC Matrix future applications:
The customer algorithm

As products and services become smarter and require less direct human intervention, customer contacts, product operation, and messaging will become more automated and programmable. Like Neil's story at the beginning of *Customer Worthy,* where his town's recreation commission publishes a message to his car's dashboard to register his children for spring baseball, messages will seek out customers through the best available channel as determined by a complex set of rules orchestrated to adapt your company's objectives to the customer's preferences, value and context.

In Neil's situation, his car was parked in a municipal lot and his family car was identified and recognized by its registration and Neil's digital footprint, which recognized that Neil's car was capable of and approved for receiving messages from the municipality.

This scenario highlights not only the use of advanced message design and communication technologies connected to customer profile databases and transaction systems, but also device-to-device interactivity where Neil's phone, laptop, and car are all "aware" and connected to the transaction, with the proximity of his laptop and phone providing sufficient authentication for the bank transaction to complete. Furthermore, the electronic payment transaction initiated when Neil said, "confirm," is likely captured and verified on the municipality's systems and executed between Neil's financial institution and the municipality directly.

Neil's successful transaction and all the steps in the transaction are also used to help the new system learn the best process route to conduct similar transactions for Neil and people like Neil in the future.

Again, all of the information exchanges, rules, and even the exchange of money and access to Neil's bank account appeared effortless and matter-of-fact to Neil due to the execution of continuously learning customer algorithms running in the background.

---

al·go·rithm (ăl'gə-rĭth'əm) n. A step-by-step problem-solving procedure, especially an established, recursive computational procedure for solving a problem in a finite number of steps.

> —*The American Heritage Dictionary of the English Language,*
> Fourth Edition, Houghton Mifflin Company, 2004.

The customer algorithm is a customer-centric formula designed to configure messages, activities and transactions to ensure customer convenience and optimum service. In the future, the customer algorithm will be the "rules center" surrounding the customer and working on behalf of the customer to ensure that only customer-worthy messages are allowed access to the customer's network.

While the customer algorithm governs access to customers on the customer's behalf, companies will continue to evolve their own algorithm—the culmination of all of the elements described in the CxC Matrix connecting advertising, sales, marketing, finance, legal, service, and operations.

Figure 12.10

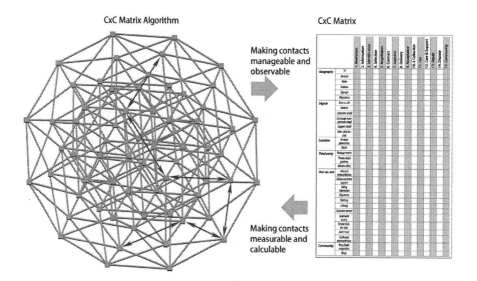

The CxC Matrix Algorithm is the mathematical expression of the probable success of each element in a contact to move the customer to the next consumer life stage factored by the customer's potential to buy anything over a specified period of time. Conversely, the CxC Matrix Algorithm is also used to calculate a customer's probability of never buying anything or failing to exceed a value threshold over the lifetime of the customer's relationship.

The elements required to construct this algorithm are available today as described in the CxC Matrix walk-through earlier in the book. Since a great number of contact elements are not yet digitized, the effort and cost to build and execute the CxC Matrix Algorithm outweighs the near term benefit except in explicitly digital channels like web-based ecommerce. As more messages become digitized and they grow their understanding of customer processes, customer networks and customer performance companies will move use of the CxC Matrix Algorithm from analytical and simulation modeling applications to real time advertising, sales, service, transaction, and communications applications.

For now, the CxC Matrix Algorithm is particularly useful in depicting customer contact scenarios as simulations to test and estimate the potential value of alternative business strategies, tactics, environmental scenarios, and competitive scenarios.

Leveraging the gaming skills of new work force

The CxC Matrix Algorithm enables companies that have completed a thorough CxC Matrix and CxC Matrix Treatment Map to efficiently experiment with alternative strategies and tactics in a manner similar to a role-based video game where multiple parties can collaborate and compete to build best outcome or highest scoring opportunities. Companies can evaluate the costs and benefits of new market entries, new product lines, mergers and acquisitions, and new product and service features from a customer performance perspective.

Customer ignorance is not an option

Companies that lack customer performance knowledge and foresight will (expensively) pursue the wrong customers with the wrong messages delivered at the wrong time through the wrong channels.

Legacy management structures, reporting systems, analytical methods and traditional decision making silos will not survive in this new competitive frontier where the best prescribed offers are designed to laser target customer's specific needs and context while surgically eliminating competition from consideration.

In the current reality where almost any company can quickly replicate another's products and services and hijack its marketing message and value propositions, you need to ensure your contacts are customer worthy at each point that proves to be critical to growing customer value.

Every employee, partner, stakeholder, shareholder, and market influencer must measure every business decision with the same single criteria: **is it customer worthy?**

Index

About the Author

MICHAEL R. HOFFMAN is a pioneer in monetizing customers and customer experience. He has spent more than 20 years working with global data and technology companies helping them design and sell systems to help companies better understand, target, win, and grow customers.

Mr. Hoffman speaks the language of sales, operations, finance and technology all with a customer dialect. His "customers are everyone's business" approach invigorates employees across a company spurring innovation, enthusiasm and a contagious passion to build, sell and deliver customer worthy solutions.

Mr. Hoffman's knowledge comes from years spent in front of customers and board rooms, within customer technology development skunk works, and inside multi-thousand cubicle customer contact centers. He shows companies how to gain unfair competitive advantage leveraging customer information to design, execute and measure superior customer worthy solutions.

In 2004, he launched Client x Client, LLC, a consulting firm specializing in marketing technology, customer relationship management (CRM), and strategy. His model for optimizing customer value is the basis for *Customer Worthy: Why and How Everyone in Your Organization Must Think Like A Customer*. He is a frequent speaker and author for the marketing, sales, CRM and technology industries and trade magazines.

His prior experience includes executive positions at Google (formerly DoubleClick), Sitel (formerly ClientLogic), Experian, and marketing technology start-ups. His diverse clients and partnerships include well-known establishments in the retail, banking, insurance, non-profit, telecommunications, publishing, travel, technology, services, and entertainment industries. His CxC Matrix is used by both business-to-consumer and business-to-business enterprises.

Mr. Hoffman is a graduate of LaSalle University and did post-graduate work at New York University and Seton Hall University. He lives in Basking Ridge, New Jersey.